The RETAIL MANAGER'S Guide to CRIME & LOSS PREVENTION

Protecting Your Business from Theft, Fraud and Violence

Liz Martínez

Foreword by Robert P. Woerner, Lt., NYPD (Ret.)

Looseleaf
Law Publications, Inc.

43-08 162nd Street
Flushing, NY 11358

www.LooseleafLaw.com   800-647-5547

Library of Congress Cataloging-in-Publication Data

Martinez, Liz.
    The retail manager's guide to crime and loss prevention : protecting your business from theft, fraud and violence / Liz Martinez ; foreword by Robert P. Woerner.
    p.cm.
Includes index.
ISBN 1-889031-66-6
1. Retail trade--Security measures. I. Title.
HF5429.27.M368 2004
658.8'7'00684--dc22

2004002391

Cover design and photo by
Mick Andreano (mickadesign.com)

DEDICATION

For Chris Koth, my wonderful son. I'm so glad you chose me at the Mom Store.

For Jeff Robles, the most fabulous man on the planet. I'm so happy you found me.

For Mario Robles, a talented and good-natured young man with a budding show business career. Break a leg!

For Sarah Cortez, the best poet in the world. Thanks for your advice, support and friendship.

And for Maggie Matthews, who trudges beside me on the road to happy destiny. You're the best friend I could ever have.

I love you all.

TABLE OF CONTENTS

FOREWORD

The basic concepts of crime prevention haven't changed much since prehistoric times. The first caveman to roll a rock in front of the cave opening discovered the concept of access control; likewise the first person to use a lighted torch to keep away intruders (animal and human) discovered security lighting. Later on, it was found that geese kept in the yard around the home would make an awful racket at the approach of strangers: the first burglar alarm system.

It doesn't take a lot of expertise in the security field to be able to implement good crime prevention techniques in the retail environment. Retailers who lack technical expertise in this field will find the information in this book easy to understand and, most importantly, easily put into practice. The ideas presented reflect basic concepts that have historical roots dating back to earliest mankind.

Today's retail security texts are written for the security professional. They are full of technological jargon that often discourages the intended end-user, the store owner and manager, from reading them. This book is written and designed to be used by the owners and managers of today's retail industry. It is not overly technical and, like today's computer programs, you will find that the format is user-friendly.

What this book focuses on is basic concepts that are important. Retailers need concern themselves only with that part, leaving the complicated psycho-social reasons behind crimes that are committed in the retail environment to criminologists.

Additionally, you will find in this book helpful strategies on hiring employees and supervision from a security perspective. Safety in the workplace is also discussed. Important to note for retailers is their responsibility in terms of workplace violence. This book discusses this issue with an eye toward preventing violence that not only endangers employees but mars the good name of the retailer. By following the guidelines laid out here, you can limit your liability for negligence should an incident occur.

Issues that affect the retailer's economic life are covered. Burglary, robbery and shoplifting are the bane of the retailer. These concerns are smartly covered in this book. The strategies outlined here are easy to implement and reduce the fear of crime.

Nearly twenty years ago, I was certified as a Crime Prevention Specialist by the New York City Police Department and eventually became the Commanding Officer of the Crime Prevention Division. Over these years I have had interaction with retailers on a local and citywide basis. My experience has shown me that if retailers had had access to this book, they would have been far less likely to be a victim of crime. As a security professional I was surprised to see how little crime prevention information there was available to the retailer. This book goes a long way to fill that void. Any and all information derived from reading this book will give the retailer that much needed edge to deter and deny the criminal element.

The wise retailer will read this book carefully and glean from its pages the ideas and concepts that will make the work environment a safer place for them, their employees and their customers.

The watchword here is *SECURITY IS EVERYBODY'S BUSINESS*.

Robert P. Woerner

Lieutenant NYPD (Ret.)

ABOUT THE AUTHOR

L iz Martínez, who has more than a decade of executive-level management experience with several leading retail chains, has been a prominent figure in the retail security industry for nearly 15 years. She is the retail security columnist for *Security Technology & Design* magazine and a frequent contributor to *Security Director*, the official publication of the New York City Chapter of the prestigious ASIS International (American Society for Industrial Security), of which she is also a member.

In addition to having served for five years as an auxiliary officer with the New York City Police Department, Martínez's diversified background includes investigatory work with New York's Administration for Children's Services and the Fairfax County (Virginia) Adult Detention Center. She also holds membership in the International Association of Marine Investigators.

Martínez's articles are seen in leading law enforcement publications nationwide and she remains active in the Police Writers Association. She is an adjunct professor of Security Management at New York's Interboro Institute, where she has made innovative enhancements to the security studies program. Martínez, who completed post-graduate studies for a Master's Degree at Seton Hill University in Pennsylvania, was also awarded a B.A. in Criminal Justice with honors from John Jay College of Criminal Justice in New York. She can be reached through her web site at www.retailsecurity.biz for consultations or to arrange training sessions.

AUTHOR'S NOTE

Congratulations on taking the first action toward keeping your store as profitable as it can be: picking up this book. Chances are, if you're reading this, you're a retail store owner or manager. Or you may be a security professional or student trying to get a handle on the unique challenges that retail operations present. Whichever category you fall into, you will find these pages packed with practical, effective measures that can be implemented to prevent or minimize the effects of store crime.

Who Should Read This Book?

One of the most frequently overlooked retail management responsibilities is security. Often, it is tempting to conclude that security is "someone else's" job: the police, mall security, in-store loss-prevention officers, and so on. But as an owner or manager, retail crime directly affects *you* by decreasing your store's bottom-line profits, thus cutting into your – and your employees' – salaries and bonuses. Criminal activity that occurs in your store carries hidden costs that take money out of *everyone's* pockets.

So everybody from the most senior manager to the newest part-time employee has a stake in security as well as a responsibility to protect profits by thwarting store crime.

What This Book *Won't* Do

While it doesn't hurt to know *why* people commit crimes, especially the kinds of criminal acts you're likely to encounter in a retail setting, the truth is that you may never find out why your store is victimized by a particular criminal. The purpose of this book is not to address the *whys* of retail crime, but to tell you about the *hows* and – more importantly – what you can do about them.

The library shelves are filled with reference texts about crime and criminality. If you want to find out more about why people commit crimes, check out some of the volumes that address those topics. You'll probably discover that no two "experts" agree on the reasons behind criminal activity, but it can be interesting reading all the same.

Profit: Retailing's Ultimate Goal

The ultimate goal in the retail arena is – first, last and always – to turn a profit. At first, it may seem difficult to justify incurring additional expenses for security because security is invisible and doesn't directly *make* money.

It's always hard to quantify a negative. In other words, it's tough to know how much money you're saving by *not* being ripped off.

Instead, because you're trying to estimate something that *hasn't* happened – sort of like the dog that didn't bark – you might try thinking in terms of how much of your profit you are willing to *give* away.

If someone walked into your store and asked you to please turn over a percentage of your profit to them, would you do it? What if they sneaked in and took your profit without your knowledge? Would that be easier to swallow? Or how about if you were told at gunpoint to hand it over? Would that make it easier for you to decide?

By not taking preventive measures against retail crime, you're doing just that – handing over your hard-earned money to criminals. Now, decide how much you are willing to give them. Is 50 percent too much? How about 20 percent? Is even 2 percent more than you're willing to share with law-breakers?

If you decide to take no security action, in effect, you are telling criminals that you're perfectly happy to let them walk off with $20 for every $1,000 you ring up. (Retail businesses lose approximately 2 percent of earnings to shrinkage.)

Some statistics have been compiled about the cost vs. the savings of a solid loss-prevention plan. They offer a useful peek at the business realities experienced by those retailers who implement loss control strategies – and those who do nothing.

When John Deere was in the business of insuring auto, boat, and other kinds of dealerships, they partnered with the businesses they insured by offering them information and suggestions to follow to reduce shrink through a program they called Riskmaster®. The head of the loss control division performed yearly comparisons of the top 10 clients (those who had the least number of insurance claims, or none at all) and the bottom 10 clients (those with the highest number of claims) in each territory, so that the entire United States was examined. Year after year, it was obvious that there was a clear difference: *the retailers who took no action toward preventing retail crime had between 100- and 200-percent more losses than the ones who implemented simple prevention procedures.*

This survey was conducted annually for many years, and the figures were consistent each time. Although every retail business is different, and various factors come into play for each, the comparison is an excellent illustration of how businesses benefit by taking steps to prevent crime. Simply put, it says that retailers who implement simple loss-control programs file half as many or fewer insurance claims than those who choose to do nothing about retail crime – and the survey looks only at insurance claims *filed*. It doesn't even take into account the number of incidences that the businesses may have experienced but not reported to the insurance company. However you look at these numbers, they paint a grim picture for the retailer who sits back and takes no action toward crime prevention.

Another way to look at the loss/profit equation is the Rule of 33. The Rule of 33 deals with a hypothetical item of merchandise that sells for $100. The wholesale cost of this item is approximately $45, which leaves $55 as the amount of gross profit. Subtract another $28 for uncontrollable expenses, plus $15 for controllable expenses. The net profit at this point is about $12. Now, deduct another $9 for taxes, and the grand total of the net profit on this $100 item is $3 (after taxes).

To put this equation into perspective, when you sell one of these $100 items, you have generated a bottom-line profit of $3. If someone steals one of these $100 items, its theft represents a bottom-line loss of $97 because the stolen item costs the same as the item you sold. So in order to make up the money you lost when the $100 item was shoplifted, you have to sell another 33 of this same item before you will realize your first penny of bottom-line net profit.

So the lesson of the Rule of 33 is that *it's 33 times more important (to your bottom line) to prevent a loss than it is to make a sale.* When you consider the costs of security in light of the Rule of 33, they become much easier to swallow.

Fortunately, there are some very effective measures you can take for a minimal investment – or for no cost at all. All you need to do is to spend a little time assessing your individual needs, then implementing the changes necessary to protect your store against unnecessary loss.

Not the Captain of Your Own Ship

Every reader is in a different situation. You may not be the person who has the final say about which security steps are taken in your store. Even if you are the big cheese who makes all the important decisions, you may be hampered in taking all the actions you want by various factors such as existing store layout, mall policies, business district requirements, and so forth. You may also feel a bit overwhelmed by all the new information you're absorbing.

To eliminate any frustrations you might encounter, this book is written in a user-friendly manner. It's written for you, the retail owner or manager, so no assumptions are made about any previous security training you might have had. It starts from the ground up so that you can derive the maximum benefit. Plus, each chapter is set up to work independently. So you can pick and choose which topics you need to address and in which order you want to tackle them.

Remember that *every* step you take toward more effective store protection means more money directly in *your* pocket. So everything you do is a positive action that will bring you closer to your desired goal of profitability.

I wish you the best of luck as you start down this new road on your continuing journey toward profitable retailing.

Liz Martínez

INTRODUCTION

A Definition of the Problem

As a retail owner or manager, you've probably noticed that store security is often either non-existent or treated as though it were not part of management's responsibilities. Sometimes retail security issues are ignored because managers feel that "someone else" should be in charge of them, or because no one in a management position really knows anything about crime prevention.

Many times, people won't take any action because it can be scary to make decisions about security without the background to know whether they're good, cost-effective choices. Or perhaps no one in your organization has been the victim of a business crime, so it's easy to believe that nothing needs to be done in terms of security. Besides, investigating security equipment and procedures can seem like a monumental task to anyone without security training or exposure.

Store managers who work for large corporations also find themselves at the mercy of the decision-makers at the company headquarters who must okay any retail security plans. And although security issues such as shrinkage have always impacted retail's bottom line, many managers – as well as corporate bean counters – have simply adopted the business philosophy that considers these losses an acceptable cost of doing business.

Many retail managers look at security as a liability because it doesn't make money, and it sometimes costs money. It is difficult to measure the effectiveness of security guards, devices and techniques that save a store money because it requires looking at a negative: how many crimes *weren't* committed, how much shrink was prevented, and so on. Also, if you implement security measures that require an investment of money and/or time, they can be seen as a drain of resources. So according to this thinking, a clerk who is busy watching for shoplifters, for example, is not selling merchandise and therefore is not making money, but rather is costing money.

Where Employees Fit in the Picture

Unfortunately, retail crime is not a problem that is going to go away. Shrink has been increasing steadily over the years. Even as recently as the mid-1980s, it was not as big a problem as it is today. There are many reasons for the upward swing, and some of them can be traced directly to the country's overall economic condition. Prior to the economic downturn experienced in the mid-to-late '80s, stores could afford to employ an adequate number of floor staff. Enough workers ensured that customers were approached when they entered the store, encouraging potential shoplifters to leave before they could steal anything. Also, payroll costs were lower, enabling stores to hire older, permanent, full-time employees who were more responsible and loyal to the store.

Since then, however, retail businesses have changed their policies in reaction to economic conditions. Although wages have risen overall, retail entities, always mindful of cost, are paying low salaries in order to minimize payroll. In addition, stores have come to depend more heavily on younger, more inexperienced part-timers, who are willing to work for lower wages. Often, they are not well paid and don't receive benefits or commissions on sales. They are the first to be laid off in response to slower sales, so their loyalty to the store isn't as strong. Also, because they are in the store working fewer hours than the permanent employees, they are not so well trained.

Staffing has also been minimized because higher interest rates have forced stores to increase the amount of capital that is put into merchandise, rather than invested in payroll. Lower numbers of floor staff also mean that sales walk out the door more frequently than thieves do because customers are frequently unable to find a clerk with the keys to unlock a clothing cable or a secure display case.

The combination of these staffing policies results in high employee turnover. Thieves come out on top because, with new people constantly replacing existing floor staff, the chances are slim that a shoplifter who has already hit the store and returns will be remembered and asked to leave before stealing more merchandise. Also, any security training of employees is rendered useless if the employees aren't around to utilize it.

The Role of In-Store Loss Prevention Teams

In chain stores, managers tend to utilize members of the security team as "extra" help to fill in the gap for other, non-sales employees. Security personnel seem to be lumped in with stock and maintenance people because they are all employees not directly involved in making sales. So when a truckload of goods arrives and the department responsible for unloading it is understaffed, for example, a manager is likely to ask a security person to bring the merchandise inside the store. In addition, it makes sense from the payroll department's point of view to pay the security team the lowest possible wage and to hire part-timers so that the store does not have to pick up the cost of a benefits package. Rather than operate at full capacity, it is also cheaper to keep the security department understaffed and to pay security people to work overtime – or simply to work short-staffed.

Alternatively, some stores contract with outside firms for security services. The difficulties with these services can be that because they are selected on the basis of the lowest bid submitted, the security service has to keep wages as low as possible in order to clear a profit. These extremely low-paying jobs sometimes attract employees who have difficulty finding work: those with limited English proficiency, for example, or, in some places in the United States, those who aren't able to get a job elsewhere because of a criminal history.

Forging a Partnership with Security

Outside the retail arena, the business sector as a whole has begun to recognize the benefits that can be realized from developing a partnership between management and security. Managers of other types of businesses recognize that what impacts the firm's bottom line also has a personal effect on their bonuses, which are based on a percentage of profit. Therefore, they find that it's in their best interest to partner with security in the quest for greater profits.

Of course, the long-reaching effects of the September 11 tragedy have done a great deal to draw attention to the importance of security. Unfortunately, many businesses have limited their new security strategies to disaster planning only. Emergency readiness is a good start toward a healthy overall business security approach, but it should be considered the beginning, not the end, of security measures.

In contrast to managers of other types of businesses, corporate retailers are often forced to ignore store security issues in favor of other concerns. Visual people, who are responsible for the layout and decoration of the store, for example, often make decisions that are in direct opposition to the store's security needs, and many times store managers have no authority to override them. A Santa Claus decoration that is hung directly in front of a surveillance camera because the store designer believes that that placement will maximize sales effectively knocks out that camera for observation purposes for the duration of the holiday shopping season (which gets longer each year), and the store manager is unable to take steps to change the placement of the decoration. Likewise, the designers typically prefer that the front of a store be kept open for aesthetic purposes, forcing the register and the cashier to the back of the store and making it that much easier for shoplifters to rip off merchandise placed near the door.

It seems, however, that independent store owners and managers have a growing awareness of the important role security plays. This awareness is reflected in day-to-day budgets, operations and procedures. Security officers of varying stripes, for example, have become a growing presence. Following the urban trend, more stores in outlying areas are also investing in alarm systems, surveillance and anti-theft devices, as well as security gates. They seem to be able to strike a balance between minimal-to-non-existent procedures and more extreme measures that make it inconvenient for both thieves and customers alike to have access to the merchandise.

Setting Expectations

Independent store management takes more proactive steps regarding store security as long as those measures are inexpensive to implement. These owners and managers are more likely to call upon local or state police for a security walk-through and recommendations for improvements in their security set-up. They also put into place low-cost measures such as mirrors that expose a blind corner to view or changing the direction of every other hanger to prevent a thief from grabbing a fistful of clothing off the rack. They are also more willing to follow up the implementation of new policies and procedures by training their employees to follow them, or asking security experts for help in doing so. The mom-and-pops are more likely to recognize that establishing a zero-tolerance policy toward shoplifting is of no use unless they also provide the workers with the knowledge they need to recognize the signals that might indicate a theft and the proper steps to take to combat it.

Savvy managers are utilizing opportunities such as staff meetings to open the discussions of management's expectations of employees. Many use this time to stress their message by inviting the police department's crime prevention unit, local beat officers, state police or mall security officers to give pointers on crime prevention and distribute the training booklets and films they often make available for employee reference.

However, regardless of the size, budget or location of a retail establishment, what often occurs is that after setting good policies, the majority of retail managers do not set the expectation that *all* the employees – everyone from the maintenance worker to the window designer to the floor manager – have a responsibility for and a stake in store security. So while shoplifters pilfer and bad-check artists scam the store out of big bucks, the employees are left swiveling their heads, seeking out that elusive person who was responsible for preventing the rip-offs from taking place. And so busy are they looking for the "security person" that they fail to take note of the shoplifter who has just sashayed out of the store with the employees' bonus in a booster box.

The Solution

In order to make your store as crime-proof as it can possibly be, managers must begin with the awareness that retail crime presents a real threat to profit and the ultimate well-being and longevity of a store. The first step down the road of successful crime-fighting is awareness. Once armed with knowledge of how the retail crime monster rears its many heads, you can move on to the next step: assessing your needs. You can use each chapter in this book to guide you in determining what policies and procedures to adopt for each topic. And finally – take action. As one well-known company advises, "Just do it."

In other words, decide which actions need to be taken, establish the appropriate policies, then reassess at regular intervals. It's simple to judge the results: you'll know you are successful when your shrink rate goes down and your profits, salaries and bonuses go up.

SECTION ONE

Internal Theft

Chapter 1
ELIMINATING INSIDE JOBS

An astounding amount of retail shrinkage is attributable to employee theft. Historically, store workers have accounted for between 30 percent and 60 percent of the losses that their employers incur. While the number fluctuates, it tends to stay within that range, worsening with economic downturns, as well as other factors.

An Ounce of Prevention

Making good hiring choices is the smartest way to head off potential thieves in your organization. There are several tools that can be used when bringing in a new person, and you should avail yourself of all the resources you can. Don't yield to the temptation to hire the first person who walks in the door. Many people hire employees based on a "gut feeling" or to fill a pressing need. However, employers and managers must be aware that there are a lot of potential liabilities for making a bad hiring decision. You can avoid a lot of headaches down the road by taking the appropriate steps.

In today's litigious climate, hiring is somewhat like marriage: it's a lot easier to do than to *un*do. So if you make good choices at the outset, you remove the need to later fix mistakes that could have been averted.

To avoid inviting potential problems from a split-second hiring choices, smart managers run the appropriate pre-employment checks. While large employers have the ability to farm out in-depth background investigations to companies that specialize in these checks, there are some basics that everyone can do.

Start by resolving not to hire anyone on the spot and to give more careful consideration to potential employees. The first step is to check with references and former employers. It is often surprising what information you come up with this way. Also, people frequently tend to stay in the same line of work, so if you don't know someone the candidate has worked with, chances are that someone on your staff does. Take advantage of your connections, too – vendors and sales reps are a font of knowledge that can be easily tapped for no more than the cost of a lunch.

Consult with your attorney to be sure that it is legal in your state to ask applicants to sign consent statements on your employment applications allowing you to investigate their criminal and driving backgrounds. Speak with your local police department for the specifics of doing checks in your municipality. Look for red flags, such as convictions or drunk-driving related incidents. If the applicant has already been untruthful, or if you spot a predisposition for substance abuse or theft-related crimes, you'll want to think twice about placing this person on your payroll. On the other hand, a drunk-driving charge 10 years ago may indicate that the person just made a one-time mistake. Proceed with caution, however: laws vary on what criteria you may use in evaluating a person's record as part of the hiring process.

Pencil-and-paper honesty tests are also a tool that can be used to help you evaluate a job candidate. Several companies sell the tests, and they have the advantage of being less costly than an intensive back-ground search. They are far from fool-proof, however: smart candidates may be able to figure out the expected answers and simply put down the answers they think you want to see. To use these tests to their maxi-mum benefit, have the candidates repeat the tests in order to determine whether there are any inconsistencies that send up a red flag.

You can have potential employees take the honesty tests again when they return for interviews with other management personnel. Two heads are better than one, so it's always best to double-check yourself by having someone else in your store interview candidates as well. If the applicant meets with you and your staff two or three times before you make a job offer, you will have a better chance of heading off trouble at the pass.

You can also protect yourself by letting candidates know up front that you drug-test potential employees. Whether or not you are able to actually administer the tests will vary depending on the laws that govern your area, but such a warning will probably scare off anyone with something to hide. (Make sure to clear this approach with your attorney ahead of time, just to be sure.) Keep in mind that drug testing is an expensive proposition and is not fool-proof: Some drugs stay in the system only a short period of time, so a candidate with sufficient knowl-edge about how the tests work could swear off long enough to pass the test and get the job.

Once you have collected all the relevant information about the candidates, checked references and received input from other staff members, go with your gut feeling. If the warning bells go off, telling you that something isn't right, heed the signal even if you can't put your finger on what bothers you about the person.

Good Management

Once you bring an employee on board, your responsibilities are just beginning. There are many excellent management texts to which you can refer to keep abreast of the finer points of employer-employee relations, but there are some universal strategies you can employ to keep internal theft at bay.

If you develop a true appreciation of your employees as people and not just human money-making machines, your attitude will shine through. Get to know your workers. You don't have to become best friends with them, but by taking an interest in what goes on in their lives, you earn their loyalty. Something as simple as inquiring about how an employee's son performed on a math test or in a soccer game transforms you into a human being, rather than the representative of a cold, unfeeling corporation that can afford to lose money or merchandise to employee pilferage. People are less likely to steal from someone with whom they perceive they have a personal relationship.

By taking the time to talk with and listen to staff members, you are in a better position to spot any changes in employee behavior. It is often through detecting a change in worker habits that managers can detect possible weak links in the security fence.

Employee behavior can supply clues of dishonesty in the workplace. Look for a worker who suddenly begins coming in late or leaving early; who makes frequent trips to the rest room or parking lot; or who experiences a sudden change in cash flow – either flashing a lot of money or being constantly broke. And an employee who seems to think that he or she is so valuable that a day off, let alone a week-long vacation, is out of the question is probably suffering from more than a neurosis. Workers who won't take time off; won't leave until everyone else has gone for the day; or hog certain jobs, such as bookkeeping duties or inventory control to themselves, are sending you a signal that something shady is going on.

If you sense that something is amiss, have a talk with the employee. Communication is important to head off an employee's personal problems before they become your problems. If you value your employees, they will sense that you are questioning them out of concern rather than suspicion. People who feel valued in a work situation tend to remain honest and devoted to you.

Regardless of how long the person has worked for you or what kind of exemplary employment record he or she had previously, don't ignore the warning signs or put off investigating what's going on. Every day that you delay is another day that thieves can rip you off. Owning or managing a business has certain perks. The flip side to those privileges is the responsibility to fix problems, even when it feels uncomfortable to confront people. But that's why you get paid the big bucks. And remember, if you allow your store to continue to be victimized by criminals, you'll see those big bucks shrink down in a big hurry.

On the other hand, one of the joys of management is getting to play the good guy sometimes. You'll find that rewarding good employee performance goes a long way toward good worker relations. Give out an "Employee of the Month" award, or just treat the staff to a pizza from time to time to let them know that they are valued and appreciated. And while cash bonuses are appreciated, dinner out with the staff once in a while can mean much more to employees than simply handing them a $20 bill, clapping them on the shoulder and saying, "Good job." Sitting down with them and sharing your time over a nice meal demonstrates your appreciation more than cold cash ever could.

The ways in which you demonstrate your appreciation for your employees are limited only by your imagination. Don't hesitate to look at what your competitors are doing, either. If they have an effective employee-appreciation program in place, mimic it, adding your own twist to it to make it unique to your store. After all, you don't want to lose good employees to the business down the street because the staff perceives that the other store is a nicer place to work.

The Payroll Dilemma

A concrete way to show your appreciation for your workers is by paying them well. Setting a fair wage can be a balancing act. On the one hand, the bottom line is boosted by limiting the percentage of payroll to gross. On the other hand, if employees don't feel that they are being paid what they are worth, they are often tempted to "make up the difference" directly from the cash register or by moving your merchandise out the back door.

The rule in retail is that your employees are your best customers – but they also have the potential to be your biggest thieves. Savvy owners and managers offer their employees healthy discounts on store merchandise to prevent staff from helping themselves to an unauthorized "five-finger discount." And you're really the winner when you offer generous employee discounts: if your customers can see employees using or wearing your merchandise, your sales of those items will increase.

Good discounts also help eliminate employee resentment. If staff members see that customers can buy your merchandise for less than they can with their employee discount, they may bypass your register when getting a new item from your store.

Discounts and Damaged Goods

While you want to offer healthy discounts to your staff, there is a potential for the workers to be overly generous to themselves at the store's expense unless management has a way of controlling items that are sold to employees.

It is common practice to allow items that have been damaged, opened or displayed to be sold to employees at a discount. An employee who wants to take a shortcut to a lower price can simply open a box, place an item on "display" for two minutes, or deliberately damage it in order to qualify for the discount.

Only the owner, or a manager or supervisor, should be in the position of deciding whether an item is eligible to be sold to an employee at a discount. It should not be left up to the staff to determine which items qualify. Each item sold to employees – whether at full price or at a discount – should be documented. In addition, any and every purchase made by employees should go through a manager. It's a good idea to designate a certain time period during which employee purchases can be made. If a worker buys something during a shift, the item should be wrapped securely, tagged, and held by the manager or at the security desk until the end of the shift. Employees should not be allowed to carry purchases around the store with them.

A good way to cross-reference the discounted goods sold and the employees who purchase them is to keep a log that lists the date, the item sold, the original purchase price, the discount amount (if any), the reason for the discount, and the name of the employee who bought it. Then put a copy of the updated log into the employee's file. If the records show "damaged" goods at a discount, for example, you will know that you need to change your tracking processes, keep a closer eye on that employee, or both.

Keeping a double record involves no extra work – you're simply photocopying your log – but it allows you to track the type of merchandise that is being sold at a discounted rate. If a large quantity of the same item is going out at lowered prices, you can spot this right away. At the same time, on each occasion that you add the copy of the updated log to the personnel folder, you will see the frequency with which a particular employee is taking advantage of the discounts and the reasons that each purchased item was discounted.

Sleight-of-Hand

If a worker is determined to pilfer store merchandise, there are several tried and true methods that may be employed. Knowing about them allows you to implement the necessary procedures to thwart the would-be thieves before they get a chance to clean you out.

An easy way for staff members to take small items is to simply tuck them inside a pocket, a purse, a backpack, a coat or jacket, an extra pair of "comfy" shoes kept by the register, or the like. If you make a locker available to each employee, there is no reason that any staff member should bring his or her personal items onto the sales floor. Require that any bags that must be carried in that area are see-through. If an employee wants to change shoes in the middle of the shift, the proper place to do so is in the locker room. Raincoats, overcoats, jackets and other outerwear belong in a locker or on the designated clothing rack. By offering the staff a place to keep their personal items, you eliminate an avenue for theft and, at the same time, let them know that you respect their desire to protect their belongings. Likewise, any packages they bring into the store should be checked at the security desk or left with the manager and held there for safekeeping until the end of the shift.

Another method of stealing is to conceal the merchandise in the garbage, the restroom, or another area where most people wouldn't think to look. A determined worker can drop an item into the garbage and go back for it after closing. One way to discourage this method of theft is to require that all garbage bags used must be of the see-through variety.

An employee can look innocent carrying an item from one location to another, but can duck inside a restroom or storage area and conceal it for later retrieval. Any hiding place will do temporarily, such as above the ceiling tiles or inside a cabinet.

Management should keep an eye out for items that belong to one area but are found in another part of the store. While they might be there for legitimate purposes, they also might be en route to a hiding place by an unscrupulous employee. Merchandise that should be elsewhere but is found behind a counter or register area could be in place, waiting for an employee's accomplice to show up and take the goods out of the store.

On the other hand, some workers are brazen, hiding their deeds in plain sight by walking out of the store with merchandise in the middle of a shift, rather than at closing or during a break. Who would think to question them in the middle of the day? You should. The employee may be making an unauthorized transfer of goods to the trunk or back seat of his or her vehicle.

For the same reason, employees should not be allowed to park near the side or rear doors or the loading dock. Designate one door as the official entry/exit location, and post a manager or security guard there to observe all personnel entering and leaving the premises. This strategy makes it harder for employees to leave with undetected stolen goods.

Inventory

Thefts of larger amounts of merchandise are often limited to senior management personnel, whose responsibilities encompass inventory control. However, employees at any level can find ways to steal goods, especially if management makes it easy for them.

Owners or managers may want to do their employees the favor of ordering certain equipment or merchandise directly from wholesalers for personal use. This is a painless way to show consideration to your employees, but you must keep a sharp eye out to make sure that you are not being more generous than you had intended. If you don't monitor the ordering process, some employees will order the goods for themselves, then "forget" to reimburse the store. The store pays the wholesaler's bills without question because they come from a regular supplier.

Be sure to reconcile the bills with the order forms to make sure that "extra" items aren't slipping through. Also, require the employee who wants to take advantage of wholesale ordering to place the order through a supervisor – not by himself or herself. It is a good idea to have the employee pay for the item upon ordering it so that you don't have the hassle of playing bill collector with your own staff when the goods arrive.

Likewise, generous retailers may want to extend the courtesy of allowing employees the personal use of store equipment, such as a computer, audio-visual equipment, and so forth, on a temporary basis. If you don't keep track of who took what and when, you will soon find that expensive items walk out and never come back. The employee who takes the item may not have dishonest intentions – he or she may legitimately forget that they have it, for example – but the loss to the store is the same as if the theft were deliberate. To avoid this problem, make sure that you have tight check-out procedures that you and the staff adhere to at all times. When recording the temporary removal of goods from the store, keep a record in the employee's file as a cross-reference.

For senior employees with more authority and autonomy, larger thefts are possible. A staffer with the responsibility for transferring merchandise from one store branch to another can divert those goods to himself or herself, either working alone or in collusion with another employee.

When working alone, a senior manager can prepare records of transfer of merchandise, then steal the merchandise. The originating store doesn't have a loss because there is paperwork documenting the "transfer." The store that ostensibly is receiving the goods doesn't know that there is a loss because they never requested the transfer in the first place.

A more enterprising thief will actually show up at the receiving store and hand the transfer paperwork to the manager at that location whose responsibility is to process the transferred goods. He or she explains that in the interest of time, and because he or she is a thoughtful person, he or she has just personally delivered the merchandise to the receiving area.

The owner, other managers, or accounting personnel should have the responsibility to reconcile all transfer paperwork to prevent or detect thefts of this sort. Also, there should be a requirement that the stock receiver must sign all transfer paperwork to verify delivery.

Another red flag is the thoughtfulness of this manager. Once or twice might be legitimate, but any employee who is consistently overly considerate warrants suspicion as to his or her motives. Hey, nobody's *that* nice!

Of course, it's easier for two people to steal, so if the manager has a partner in crime, transfer thefts are easier to engineer. The originating store's manager makes up the transfer paperwork, and the receiving store manager, who is colluding with the first manager, signs for the merchandise as though it were legitimately received. The two then split the goods. Again, the loss is transferred to another branch.

Transfers can also be used to cover up the theft of lost or stolen merchandise after the fact. During World War II, U.S. Navy personnel in charge of supply perfected this method of accounting for lost items. When a ship sank, every piece of equipment that could not be accounted for anywhere in the Navy was reported to have gone down with the ship. One former Navy man confessed that in at least one case, if everything that was reported as being lost when the ship sank had actually been loaded onto it, the ship would have been so weighed down that it would have sunk in the harbor before even getting out to sea!

If fake transfers are being used to conceal theft, that's a bad situation. If the problem is that so much merchandise is being lost or unaccounted for, that false transfer paperwork is created to hide the fact, that's almost worse. Either way, it's a signal that management needs to be strengthened, store procedures desperately need an overhaul, and personnel may also need to be replaced if they demonstrate that they are unable to follow the rules.

One way to spot these losses before they destroy your business is by taking inventory regularly, both on a planned and a spot-check basis. Planned inventories are necessary at regular intervals for various business reasons, but of course, thieves on the payroll know when to expect them and can make plans to cover up any shortages in advance. Surprise inventories are more likely to catch shortages that dishonest personnel don't have time to conceal. Likewise, employees know when to expect regular scrutiny of store paperwork and accounting books, perhaps at the end of each month. Doing an unannounced audit can also reveal problems in those areas.

Depending on the size of your operation and your budget, you may be able to hire an outside inventory company. The independent company supplies the workers, who are trained to take inventory of many different kinds of products. Many times they will be armed with a scanner and will go through your store at lightning speed, electronically counting items. The advantage of using an outside company is that their workers are unknown to your employees, and thus the opportunity to cover up any shortages is limited.

If you must use your own staff to take inventory, have the members of one department take inventory for another. Allowing workers to inventory their own merchandise makes it easier for the dishonest ones to cover up missing items. Be aware, too, of the relationships between members of departments. If two managers often have their heads together, make sure that neither one of them is responsible for inventorying the other's area. While they may just be good friends, you can reduce their opportunity to cover up losses in the other's department.

Be sure that the managers who prepare for the arrival of the inventory service have a thorough understanding of how merchandise is counted. If a delivery is received just before inventory, for example, and the invoice is included with current paperwork, but the shipment itself is held to the side so that it can be processed once things calm down, that merchandise will show up as a shortage. Also, the invoices for back-ordered items must be scrutinized to ensure that an item that hasn't actually been received yet is considered received in error. You can spend a lot of time, energy and money trying to fix inventory shortage problems that don't exist if paperwork and tracking procedures aren't adhered to.

Lay-Away Losses

Dishonest employees can mine the lay-away field for ill-gotten gains. As with other types of employee theft, the key to remaining solvent is to establish procedures and do periodic spot-checks to ensure that employees are following them.

Thefts from the lay-away department are almost always attributable to dishonest employees, rather than to greedy customers. Employees can work in tandem with their criminal cohorts to pull off small thefts on a steady basis, or they can be a solo act, taking your merchandise on their own. Either way, there are several things you can do to prevent lay-away losses.

Making sure that merchandise that is set aside for lay-away is easily visible is a good start. If lay-away items are kept hidden, it is easier for clerks to add or disappear merchandise without management catching on. A cubbyhole arrangement, with merchandise placed in see-through containers within stacked bins or built-in "cubbys," creates a simple filing system that is also easy to inspect. The store's copy of the lay-away slip should be easily accessible so that a spot-check can be conducted quickly. The layout for the merchandise should be created in such a way that each item can be cross-referenced both numerically and alphabetically. Pre-printed lay-away slips that are numbered in sequential order help managers keep track of the transactions and make it easier to spot a missing slip.

Keeping merchandise visible can help eliminate the possibility that employees will add a few extra items to a lay-away as a "bonus" to their friends. Visible merchandise also reduces the chance that the lay-away clerk will put aside a certain amount of merchandise, yet record a lower number of items on the lay-away slip. The advantage of keeping the store copy of the lay-away slip within plain sight is that it deters dishonest workers from bagging merchandise for lay-away but not creating a slip for it because the worker is the real "customer." A readily visible lay-away slip also discourages employees from recording a lower price on the slip in order to give their friends an unauthorized discount on the merchandise, or from holding onto monies paid toward lay-away items instead of ringing up the payments and depositing the cash into the register.

Lay-away slips for merchandise that have been picked up by the customer must be turned in along with the register receipts. If the old slips aren't accounted for, employees can "recycle" them in order to move out identical merchandise that is never paid for. A manager's approval should also be required for every lay-away transaction that is canceled, voided or forfeited so that a clerk will not be able to prepare the paperwork showing that the lay-away transaction has been canceled without returning the merchandise to the floor. The manager should also supervise or personally return items previously on lay-away to the store's stock to ensure that they are not diverted by a dishonest employee or simply left behind in error. Either way, the store will show a shortage of that item unless management ensures that the proper procedures are established and adhered to by all employees.

Chapter 2
THE CASH REGISTER

There are numerous con games that cash-handling workers can play in your store, and crooked employees think up new ones every day. To keep unnecessary temptation away from employees, a system of checks and balances is necessary. Clearly defined procedures must be put into place and communicated to workers, and management must do regularly scheduled audits as well as surprise spot-checks to be sure that workers are following the rules and that opportunities to create losses are eliminated.

Written policies requiring and prohibiting certain behaviors are important. To avoid the huge task of making the rules up from scratch, check your local library or bookstore for management books that contain policies applicable to many types of businesses. Incorporate only those sections that are appropriate for your store.

Once you put the handbooks together, distribute a copy to each worker and have everyone sign an agreement to abide by store rules. Make no secret of the consequences for infractions – including prosecution. If an employee does commit a crime against the store, follow through with legal proceedings. Having a policy you don't enforce simply invites workers to violate it.

Handling Voids

Transactions can be voided for a number of legitimate reasons: the customer does not have enough money to pay for the purchase; the customer forgot his or her wallet; the customer changed his or her mind after the sale is rung up; the customer's check or credit card was not approved; or the proper discount was not applied to a purchase.

"Creative" employees can use a void as an additional source of ill-gotten income. Fraudulent voids are committed when a cashier rings up a purchase, accepts the money for it, then voids the transaction in the register and pockets the money. Alternatively, a dishonest cashier can pick up a discarded register receipt, mark it "Void," slip it into the register, and remove the equivalent amount of cash. In either scenario, the register tape will tally with the amount of cash in the drawer at the end of the day.

To prevent employees from using voids as a way of stealing from the register, a manager or supervisor should be required to approve any voided transactions by initialing the register tape, filling out a void form, or both. Any voided transaction should be approved by management in the customer's presence.

In addition, require that receipts be stapled to the bags or otherwise affixed to purchases in order to prevent loose ones from floating around and offering an easy opportunity for theft. A sign posted on all registers offering customers a sum of money – say, $5 – if a receipt is not presented at the time of purchase helps keep cashiers diligent about giving out receipts.

Refund Control

Like voids, refunds are fertile grounds for theft. An employee can work with a friend who brings in an item and is issued a refund that is later split with the dishonest worker. Or an employee can make fraudulent refunds on his or her own by removing the cash from the register and writing up a refund form, listing as the recipient a fake person at a fictitious address. Alternatively, employees can randomly choose the purchase records of a real customer and process a refund – which is taken by the employee.

As with other cash management functions, a manager or supervisor must authorize and countersign any refunds. Sequentially numbered refund vouchers should be maintained in a refund file for perusal at regular intervals. All transactions of an employee who is responsible for the lion's share of the refunds should be scrutinized to determine whether some or all of them are fraudulent. Any vouchers that are processed out of sequence should also be double-checked to ensure that employees are not falsifying a manager's signature.

A good supervisory technique that does double-duty as refund verification and customer service is to follow up with mail and/or phone calls inquiring about the customer's experience. A letter or post card that is sent out to all customers who receive refunds can ask a few questions, such as "Was your refund handled promptly?" "Did our employees extend courteous service to you during the refund transaction?" "Would you shop in our store again?" As an incentive for the customer to respond, the store can offer a $5 coupon good toward the customer's next purchase. If the mail is returned because of a nonexistent address or because no one with that name lives at the address, it is an indication that something is fishy and that further investigation should be undertaken to determine whether the refund is legitimate.

Likewise, managers or supervisors should pull refund vouchers out at random intervals and call the recipients. If they profess not to know anything about having received refunds, something is definitely wrong. If the refunds are legitimate, it offers managers an opportunity to impress upon the customers how important their business is to the store.

Sweethearting

Sweethearting at the cash register refers to a cashier who rings up sales for friends or family members, but does not charge the full price for these favored customers. Sweethearting is accomplished in several ways. Cashiers can ring up only one item out of several identical ones that are presented; they can ring up only the lower-priced items that are presented and fail to charge for the higher-priced ones; or they can manually override the prices of the items they do ring up.

Managers should look at all price overrides recorded at the end of each shift. If one cashier is responsible for many overrides, that cashier may be sweethearting. Alternatively, the overrides may signal that an item was incorrectly priced or that the wrong price was entered into the computerized register system.

A good policy to prevent sweethearting at the register is not to allow a cashier to ring up purchases for his or her own family or friends.

Cash Theft Methods

Stealing cash is the most profitable method of theft for employees because there's no waiting period to use it, as there might be if they fence stolen goods, and it's untraceable. Cash is cash no matter where it originates, and it spends the same everywhere.

The easiest way for an employee to take cash is to do simply that – just remove it from the register and slip it into a pocket or purse. This method should also be the easiest to detect. If a particular employee's cash drawer is always short, that's a sign that the employee may be removing money in an unauthorized way. However, if there is only one register to which all employees have access – known as a "universal till" – then it may be harder to trace the origin of the shortages.

One way to control cash theft from a universal till is to assign a cashier to the register at the beginning of a shift. That person should count the drawer and sign for the money. At the end of the shift, the dedicated cashier should present the drawer to a supervisor, who should count the money and sign off on the total. If the drawer comes up short when one particular person is responsible for the register, it may be a sign of theft.

Another way that cashiers can steal is to short-change a customer. But enterprising cashiers can also short other cashiers or supervisors when getting change for the register. Any short-changing will show up at the end of the day, when registers are balanced. Again, a pattern of losses may indicate who is causing the cash shortages.

Markers, Under Rings, and Unrecorded Sales

More sophisticated thieves who steal from the register will try to cover up the shortages. One way that cashiers can take money yet still balance at the end of the day is by under ringing sales. The cashier rings up an item for less than its cost, but charges the customer the full price and pockets the difference.

Likewise, a cashier can ring up a no-sale (open the drawer without keying in a purchase), take the money from the customer, and keep it instead of putting it into the register.

Creative cashiers can use "markers" to keep track of the amounts they are stealing. A marker can be a foreign object, such as a bobby pin or a paper clip, or it can be a coin that is slipped into the wrong tray. Each thief has his or her own system. For one person, each bobby pin may correspond to $5 and each paper clip may represent $10. For another cashier, a penny in the quarter tray may signify a theft of $25, and a penny in the dime tray may record a $10 shortage. Whatever the system may be, the cashier will take out the appropriate amount of money at the end of the shift to ensure that the drawer tallies with the register tape.

Supervisors can spot markers by inspecting cash drawers in the middle of the day, at irregular intervals. If change is in the wrong trays, or if there are foreign objects in the cash drawer, counting out the drawer immediately will prevent the cashier from having time to remove enough cash to balance. Closing cash registers during the middle of the shift and counting the drawers on a random basis also gives management a handle on whether anything unorthodox is happening.

In addition, it is a good idea to require documentation, such as filling out a log and getting a supervisor's signature, for every no-sale transaction.

Gift Certificates

Like other paradoxes of retailing, a gift certificate is the most cost-effective sale that can be made, yet it supplies one of the easiest ways for employees to steal. A gift certificate represents money received for merchandise that will be taken later on. The store gets the customer's money up front without having to provide any items in return. In the interim during which the recipient holds onto the gift certificate, the store can use the money that has already been received in any way it deems fit. Sometimes a gift certificate is purchased, and no one ever redeems it because the recipient misplaces it or forgets about it, in which case the store keeps all the money.

A worker can sell store gift certificates to friends or associates in exchange for cash. The buyer then returns to the store and redeems the fraudulently obtained certificate for merchandise. In this case, the store has lost the entire cost of the product.

To prevent gift certificates from walking away, they should be kept in a secure place where only managers or supervisors have access to them. Numbering them sequentially and keeping a log of the name of the purchaser, the date of purchase and the method of payment are also good ways to keep track of them. Once the recipient redeems the certificate, deface it and make a notation on the log. Mutilating or marking the used certificates and keeping track of the ones that have been presented to the store for merchandise prevents employees from "recycling" them for profit.

Suspicious Behavior

Managers who are on their toes will be proactive about looking for irregularities. However, sometimes an employee's behavior tips management off that all is not well.

Any employee who hogs a cash-handling job, or who copies over balance sheets "to make them look neater" is sending a signal that his or her motives may not be pure. Likewise, a worker who refuses to take a vacation or a day off may be sticking around to cover up a pattern of thefts.

Addictions and social problems can also cause a need for extra cash. People can be addicted to alcohol, drugs, gambling, sex, food, or other things. Employees may have to pay child support or alimony, or may not be receiving payments from a spouse or ex. Any of these issues, and many others, manifest themselves in various ways, but a change in behavior is generally the common thread.

A chronic shortage of cash or sudden signs of wealth can indicate that something is not right in an employee's life. A worker who was always punctual but who now comes in late and calls in sick a lot can also be telling you that something is amiss. Other obvious signs of problems include bloodshot eyes, frantic behavior, leaving the store several times during the day, having secretive phone calls or meetings, a drop-off in work quality, mood swings, antagonistic or violent behavior or speech, bringing weapons to work, crying jags, or any other out-of-the-ordinary or unacceptable behavior.

If you spot any signs of trouble, do not wait for it to go away on its own. Many problems get much worse before they get better, and most problems do not disappear by themselves. If you wait to ask an employee about behavioral changes, you are giving the problem an opportunity to worsen – and the employee an opportunity to steal. It isn't necessary to have a huge confrontation with an employee who is exhibiting signs of trouble, but a friendly inquiry in private is certainly appropriate. Asking general questions, such as, "I notice that you're coming in late a lot. Is everything all right?" can elicit a truthful response. If the employee does not admit to having any problems and the behavior does not immediately improve, managers must begin the documentation process.

The Importance of Paperwork

Store owners and managers are like anyone else – they don't usually enjoy confrontational situations. It is tempting to wait for something overt to happen before taking action against an employee. Unfortunately, the longer you wait, the more opportunity employees have to rob you blind. You must begin the process at the first sign of trouble. An informal talk is generally the first step, followed by written reprimands. Whatever the established procedure is in your store, follow it. Keep written accounts of any discussions that take place with the employee, and record the details of any inappropriate or questionable incidents that occur at the workplace, regardless of who is involved. Desperate people will often deny and lie, and without written documentation, you have no way to establish a pattern of problematic behavior.

If your suspicions turn out to be unfounded, and the employee in question does not have a serious problem, then an informal talk is probably sufficient to nip any unwanted behavior in the bud. However, if the behavior recurs later on, keeping a record of what was discussed with the employee and when, allows you to establish that a pattern of inappropriate behavior has taken place over time. Should a government agency or an attorney step into the picture, you will have the documentation to show what occurred, when, and what efforts you made to correct the behavior. That documentation can be the difference between triumphing and being hit with fines or penalties.

Chapter 3
BANKING PROCEDURES

fter taking the appropriate steps to safeguard cash at the point of sale, nobody wants to risk its disappearance. One point of vulnerability is the bank deposit; another concerns writing checks drawn on the corporate account.

As with other types of losses in the retail arena, some may result from illegal activities, while others may be the result of poor training or employee unsuitability for a given task. Good management techniques will address both causes and prevent cash from hemorrhaging out of the business.

Divide and Conquer

As with other responsibilities that bring employees into proximity with currency, the preparation of bank deposits holds an opportunity for theft. An employee who wants to steal can do just that – take the money out of the deposit. Poof! It's gone. The question becomes how to cover it up.

If managers don't routinely examine deposit records to ensure that the figures match up with the totals on the daily cash register reports, there is nothing for a dishonest employee to cover up, because no one will ever catch on to the missing money. So periodic, unannounced comparisons of these documents is essential to keep a finger on the pulse of the store's circulatory system: its cash processes.

If managers are thorough and employees know that the records will be checked, they can still siphon out cash, then attempt to cover it up through a process called "lapping." An employee engaged in lapping skims cash from a bank deposit, then uses the same exact amount of cash from the next day's deposit to cover the shortage – and takes a little extra bonus for himself as well. The employee continues stealing day after day in the same manner. In this way, the shortages keep increasing, and the only clue to the theft is that there appears to be a lag in the time it takes the bank to process the store's deposits.

If employees whose responsibilities include preparation of the bank deposits refuse to take vacation time, it is a signal that something is amiss. Workers who are up to no good, and who are prospering from whatever theft arrangement they have created at the store, will not want to take days off for two reasons. The less important one is that time away from the store cuts into their profits. The more important motive behind showing up every day is that when replacement workers take over the cash duties, discrepancies will show up that point to the dishonest workers. Someone who is lapping, for example, can't cover up the shortages in the deposits if an honest employee takes over for even a few days.

The best way to prevent the whole scenario from occurring is to split up the cash-sensitive tasks among several employees. Cross-training workers provides for greater overall efficiency and carries the bonus of eliminating opportunities for theft.

Cash handling jobs should be assigned to employees on a rotating basis in random order. That means that if Alice, Bob, and Charlie are all trained to prepare the bank deposits, the schedule should not be set up so that Alice does it on Monday, Bob is responsible for it on Tuesday, Charlie carries it out on Wednesday, and so forth. Instead, managers should make the assignment each day, without advance notification to employees. Alice could do it on Monday and Tuesday, for example, while Charlie is assigned on Wednesday, Bob is given responsibility on Thursday, the manager does it personally on Friday, then Charlie gets it again on Saturday, and so on. The order doesn't matter as long as the pattern is not predictable.

Three Is Not a Crowd

Once the preparation strategies are in place, the money has to be transported to the bank. An employee could simply walk off with the entire deposit instead of actually going to the bank, and the loss would not be noticed unless management follows up regularly.

If managers are meticulous about tracking paperwork, then the biggest consideration regarding the deposit itself is the possibility of robbery. An easily identifiable bank bag is a juicy target for a thief. Bank bags pretty much all look alike, so the person carrying the bag should take pains to conceal it in a pocketbook or a briefcase, tuck it into the waistband of slacks or a skirt and cover it with a coat or long shirt – even tuck it into a coffee-stained paper take-out bag. Anything will do as long as the bank bag isn't in plain sight.

There is safety in numbers, so under no circumstances should one person make the deposit alone. If the bank is within walking distance, another employee should follow the one carrying the bank bag and keep an eye out for anything unusual, such as someone trailing or paying too much attention to the employee with the bag. Thieves can also work in pairs. One of them may distract the person with the bag by spilling something obvious, such as ketchup, on the person's clothing. While the bad guy is apologizing and trying to help clean up the mess – really, while he's distracting the victim – his partner steals the bank bag.

Should the employee who's following see anything go awry, he should use a cell phone to call police immediately. Taking a good look at the thieves in order to supply a description is most helpful. Also, noting whether the bad guys leave in a vehicle, and if so, its description and license number, and in which direction they flee will all be of assistance to law enforcement. Should the victim be injured, the employee with the cell phone can also use it to summon medical assistance.

If the bank is far enough away that the employee making the deposit must drive there, the second employee should follow in another vehicle. Again, the idea is to keep an eye out for trouble and to call for help should anything go wrong.

If the person with the bank bag arrives at the depository but notices that someone is loitering in the area or that there is a disturbance, such as a large crowd, or anything else that doesn't look right, it is better to come back with the money another time than to risk becoming a victim just to keep a schedule. If someone has a "gut feeling" that something is amiss, the person should honor his instincts by leaving the immediate area and calling the police at a non-emergency number to request an officer's presence while the bank drop is made. Many law enforcement personnel are happy to assist citizens who feel unsafe.

At a night depository, the employee with the bank bag should check and double-check to ensure that the bag slides all the way down the chute and does not get caught near the top, where the next person to unlock the depository could come into a windfall by snagging the first bag and keeping its contents. The following employee should observe the person making the deposit to make sure that all goes smoothly. If not, he or she can summon assistance on the cell phone.

As with deposit preparation, taking the money to the bank should be assigned to different employees on a random, rotating basis. The time the deposits are made should also vary from day to day. An enterprising thief can make off with a day's receipts simply by knowing that an employee heads for the bank every day at a certain time and intercepting the worker en route.

If there is a tremendous amount of cash that must be taken to the bank or a great number of rolls of coins that are brought back daily, then contracting with an armored vehicle transport service may be a worthwhile investment. Rolls of coins are bulky and heavy and more difficult to conceal than a bank bag containing mostly bills and checks, so more care needs to be taken to disguise them. And once the employee returns from the bank with the change, be sure that it goes in the proper place, such as a safe, immediately. Leaving a bank bag filled with rolled coins lying around the store – even for a few minutes – is an invitation to dishonest workers to help themselves.

Another problem with bank deposits can occur when employees who are relatively unsophisticated are duped by thieves. Workers should be instructed not to engage in conversation with anyone while traveling to the bank or during the process of making the deposit. Fast-talking swindlers can pull cons that sound legitimate at first, but which ultimately end up with the employee handing over the bank deposit, perhaps with a promise that the thief will return momentarily with an additional amount of money or a reward, or something else that seems beneficial to the worker. Contact local authorities for information on any con games that are taking place in your area so that you can warn employees not to fall for them.

Sometimes, however, a naïve employee can fall for a well thought out scam. In one case, thieves took a box that resembled a mailbox, but which belonged to a private package delivery service, and which was placed in an outside area so that people wishing to send packages via this service could drop them into the box after hours. The bad guys moved the box underneath the night depository at a bank and placed a hand-lettered sign above it. The sign, which was scrawled in magic marker, read, "Depository out of order. Use box below."

A young employee who was charged with making the bank deposit followed the directions and dropped the bank bag into the mailbox. The thieves came by later on and retrieved the money.

Of course, a bank would never use an insecure box to accept its customers' money, but the young employee didn't know that. In this case, the store owner or manager should have discussed the incident with the employee and reviewed the procedures for making bank deposits. Unfortunately, because management did not take the time to do this, the employee fell for the same trick again, leaving another day's deposit in the unauthorized box when the thieves repeated their scam.

Company Check-Writing Privileges

Employees who are trusted with access to the store's accounts are in a position to do a great deal of financial damage to the business. A worker who comes with good references and who does nothing to abuse the owner's or manager's trust during the initial months of employment may indeed be an honest employee – or a dishonest one just waiting for the right time to pounce.

Even employees who have a history of honesty may become dishonest under the right circumstances. The formula for an illegal activity is Crime = motive + opportunity. While you cannot control disasters or mishaps such as illness, accidents, or a spouse's layoff from a job, which may cause employees to suddenly need extra money, you can control the other end of the equation: the opportunity to steal.

The most obvious way for a worker who is allowed to write checks drawn on the company's funds to steal money is to simply write himself or herself a check. Employees who are not that bold may write a check to a friend and split the money. There may be some attempt to provide fictitious paperwork – orders, invoices, etc. – to conceal the theft, but if no one routinely inspects the books and looks at corresponding paperwork, there is no need to do even a minimal amount of concealment.

Another method of misusing company checks is by creating a "ghost" employee – one who exists only on paper. The dishonest employee writes payroll checks to the non-existent person and cashes them personally. Alternatively, the deceitful worker "forgets" to remove the name of an employee who has left the company from the payroll roster. Again, checks are cut in someone else's name, and the check writer cashes them.

Managers should occasionally check the backs of checkbooks to ensure that individual checks have not been removed out of sequence to be used for an unauthorized purpose. Blank checks should be safeguarded, as should any automatic check-writing machines, preferably in a safe. Those who are authorized to sign company checks must never sign a blank check, and any checks that are written on a regular basis should still have supporting paperwork for the expenses, rather than taking it on blind faith that the goods or services have been provided "as usual."

In accordance with good business practice, managers must check the store's accounts regularly and randomly to ensure that everything balances. If a discrepancy is uncovered, an investigation needs to be instituted, rather than taking an employee's word that the inconsistency is due to a "clerical error." Managers must make sure that employees with account access take time off regularly, and workers should be cross-trained and accounting duties rotated on an irregular basis.

SECTION TWO

External Theft

Chapter 4
SHOPLIFTING

While employees can be a source of theft, outsiders also contribute to store losses. The most dreaded source of shrinkage is the shoplifter. Shoplifters come in all shapes, sizes, ages, races and genders. They may look like your grandfather or your next-door neighbor, or they may resemble someone in a scary prison movie – or a Girl Scout. The only way you can be sure that someone is a shoplifter is if you see the person leaving with merchandise that is not paid for.

Employees: Your Eyes and Ears

Floor employees are the first line of defense against shoplifters. Although a shoplifter can be anybody, workers are the ones who are in a position to spot someone who looks as though he or she doesn't fit in with the store or the area.

An example of a person who doesn't fit in would be someone who is wearing an overcoat in the middle of July. That person may not be in the store to buy, but may be using the large coat to conceal stolen merchandise.

Beware of making assumptions, however. While a high-end store that sells expensive merchandise, for example, would naturally attract customers who could afford to purchase such items, it would be a severe error in judgment to assume that because a person is not wearing designer clothing, he or she is there to steal. The scene in the movie *Pretty Woman* illustrates this kind of incorrect assumption: The fact that Julia Roberts' character is dressed in a way that implies that she can't afford to buy anything in an expensive clothing store belies the fact that she's carrying a handful of hundred-dollar bills and is ready to spend them.

Likewise, store owners, managers, employees and contractors cannot afford to make the mistake of assuming that a person is a shoplifter based solely on that person's race. Doing so can buy the store a lot of trouble in the form of an expensive lawsuit.

Other than someone who doesn't fit in, employees should look for a person who appears nervous or ill at ease. Shoplifters are often more interested in store personnel than in the merchandise. Upon entering the store, a legitimate customer will take in the layout to determine which areas to browse first. A shoplifter's priority is to scope out how many employees are working and where they're situated in order to determine the best places to steal without being observed. By requiring that a staff member greet everyone who walks in the door, you will increase your security immensely. The second an employee catches a shoplifter's eye and lets the person know that the employee will help him in just a moment, a smart thief will scurry for the exit. Thieves don't want anyone to be able to identify them.

Another clue that someone may be in the store to steal is that shoplifters frequently fail to examine the merchandise they have in their hands at any given moment. While customers who intend to buy will look at products they are holding, shoplifters are more interested in scouting around to see whether store personnel are watching them.

Employees should also be aware that shoplifters sometimes shuttle back and forth between the same areas because they are getting ready to steal merchandise. They "shop" for the items they're planning to steal, leave the area, then return to remove merchandise from its packaging, stack items together to make a smaller bundle, or remove tags.

Likewise, people who linger or appear to be just hanging around may be casing the store, waiting for an opportunity to steal. If they touch a lot of merchandise but don't seem inclined to purchase anything, that is another tip-off that they may be planning to shoplift. People who stay near counters that are close to the exits may also be preparing to grab something from a display and head for the door, where a partner-in-crime may be waiting to spirit them away in a vehicle.

The Power of Customer Service

The best way to combat shrink and make sales is by ensuring that the staff provides excellent customer service. Legitimate shoppers appreciate the attention, while shoplifters don't like it in the least and may leave to find another stealing ground where they won't be noticed.

Attentive employees can thwart potential thieves simply by doing their jobs well. If possible, designate staff members to greet customers at the door. Encourage floor employees to move around the store, rather than staying in one spot. By circulating, workers have a better idea of what is going on and will discourage shoplifters who are afraid of getting caught by an eagle-eyed staff member. If workers are around, smiling and making themselves available to customers, shoppers who want to try on a garment or ask questions about an item will be able to do so easily, which leads to increased sales. It also helps reduce shrink because shoplifters don't like to be approached or identified. Being noticed by workers makes it difficult for thieves to steal. They don't want anyone to remember their faces or descriptions later on, when merchandise turns up missing. If they are collecting merchandise in one spot in order to steal it all at once, an employee is in a good position to notice their activities and approach them, which will encourage them to leave quickly.

In-Store Protection

Because it's easiest for a thief to get away fast with merchandise that is displayed near an exit, the more expensive items should be kept toward the rear of the store and away from the exit doors. If high-ticket merchandise is kept near a front door, it is also easy for thieves to come back when the store is closed and pull a "smash-and-grab" – smash the window and grab the merchandise. Ideally, high-value goods should be kept locked up, with only samples displayed in locking cases or secured to racks.

Merchandise should be kept in order at all times, so that if something is missing, employees can spot the empty space immediately – perhaps in time to thwart the thief's escape from the store. All staff members must be kept abreast of sales and price changes, especially part-time workers, who are more likely to be out of the loop when it comes to changes in store policies. Everyone should know the retail costs of items at all times so that dishonest shoppers cannot get away with switching price tags or other games designed to rip off the business.

It should be a top priority to ensure that computers are updated with the correct prices and that staff members are familiar with price changes so that customers don't get a free ride because an old price was inadvertently left unchanged in the system. Also, it is very important to make sure that your signage always displays the correct prices. If you leave a sale sign on the floor advertising that a particular item is being sold for $20, for example, you must sell it to the customer for $20, regardless of the fact that the sale ended yesterday and today's price is supposed to be $30. Even if the sign remained posted in error, it is considered an illegal tactic to advertise one price, yet charge the customer a higher price. As soon as an error like this is brought to your attention, smile, sell the item to the customer for the advertised price, remove the sign, and have a discussion with the employee who was supposed to have taken the sale signs down. Some customers who know that you must sell an item at the advertised price will look for an opportunity to physically move a sale sign from one area to another for the sole purpose of forcing the store to sell them a more expensive item at a lower price. If your floor staff is alert, they won't get the opportunity to pull any sign switching.

Visibility is also an important consideration. Aisles should be designed so that cashiers and clerks have the maximum view of what is happening in the store. If large displays block employees' view of certain areas, shoplifters will take advantage of the limited visibility to steal products from those areas, banking on not being observed by store staff. In addition to keeping displays low, nothing should be mounted high on walls in front of any type of observation device, such as a camera or mirror. Once the device is blocked, it is effectively rendered useless, and store security is compromised.

Cash registers should be located in the front of the store or just inside exit doors. This positioning forces everyone leaving the store to go past the cashier, making the register hard to bypass without paying. If someone does make a run for it with stolen merchandise, the cashiers are in an excellent position to get a description of the person.

Security guards are another option in the arsenal of shoplifting prevention tools. There are pros and cons to employing or contracting for guards. Having uniformed guards in the store may discourage kids and amateur thieves, but professional shoplifters will not be fazed by their presence. It is also easy for workers to be lulled into a false sense of security when guards are around, leading them to be less observant of what's going on around them. The most important thing to remember is that *Security is Everybody's Business*, so if guards are on the premises, it is not "their" job to prevent shoplifting – that responsibility still lies with all employees.

If you do employ professional security agents, posting uniformed guards at the exits is a good deterrent, and having plainclothes detectives, or "floorwalkers," circulating among shoppers adds to the overall effectiveness of the security effort.

Keep in mind that if you use security officers – whether they are store employees or contract workers supplied by an agency – their behavior will reflect directly on you. If they are courteous and well groomed, that enhances the store's reputation. On the other hand, if the guards are not well trained, or if they do not follow procedure and illegally search or detain someone, you are also responsible for that. The store owner is the one who will be sued for damages if the offended party chooses to seek a legal remedy. As with most things, the quality of guard you get will depend, at least in part, on the amount you are willing to pay. If you offer higher wages or agree to give an agency a higher rate, you can demand more qualified personnel.

One alternative to employing live security guards that has had good results in deterring shoplifting in some overseas markets involves using cardboard cutouts of police or security officers. Especially during the holiday season, when more shoppers – and thus, more thieves – patronize retail establishments, some stores have found that placing life-size cardboard likenesses of a uniformed officer in strategic spots around the store reduces thefts. A variation on the life-size model is a head-and-shoulders cardboard photographic representation. It might also be worthwhile to try your own variations on this method, such as a mannequin that is decked out in an official-looking uniform, or even a poster depicting an officer that presents an anti-crime message.

When potential shoplifters glance around and spot a lifelike depiction of a person in uniform, they often abandon their plans to steal, just as though a real officer were present. Such inanimate "officers" can be effective deterrents to shoplifters in places such as fitting rooms, where a real cop wouldn't stand and watch customers, or to supplement the live security officers already in place. It has been shown, however, that the effectiveness of these cardboard likenesses diminishes with repetition. If you do choose to use this method of deterrence, don't use it too often, and constantly rotate the placement of the cutouts.

For more information about crime prevention methods that have been successful in your area, assistance is often available from a number of different sources. Your mall security supervisor, local beat police officer, or a representative from the state police will often be eager to come to the store to give employees crime prevention strategies and tips. Frequently, they will be able to provide training booklets or films. It is in their interest to help you prevent crime because lower crime rates on their beats make them look good. Local and national merchant associations are also a good source of crime prevention information, and they often provide it free of charge or as part of the materials supplied when you join the organization.

Apprehending a Thief

Laws vary about what is required in order to take someone into custody for shoplifting. In some places, the thief must leave your premises to demonstrate an intent to steal. In others, concealment laws allow you to detain someone for secreting your merchandise out of sight. What remains consistent from place to place, however, is the danger involved in making an apprehension.

Danger comes into play not only on a physical level, but also on a legal level. A shoplifter may be a deranged person or someone stealing to feed his or her drug habit, and may react violently to being apprehended. If you or your employees detain a suspect in an improper manner, you could be sued, found liable and forced to pay the shoplifter for damages! This is a very real danger, and thieves know it. In fact, some of them deliberately commit what looks like shoplifting, but then engage in some sleight of hand so that the merchandise is not found on them – solely to make money from you in court.

Depending on where your store is located, the laws governing detention of a shoplifter will differ; however, there are three points of similarity that remain constant:

- You or your employee must personally witness the act of shoplifting occur. A report from a witness, such as a customer, is useless in this case.
- You or your employee must keep in sight the shoplifter and the place that the shoplifter concealed the merchandise (coat, stroller, etc.) constantly, without any lapse in view whatsoever, even for a second, in order to be dead certain that the thief still has the goods in his possession.
- The shoplifter must do something that indicates that he has the intent to steal. Depending on your jurisdiction, that act may include ripping off a price tag, concealing the merchandise, or actually exiting the store without paying.

Civil suits are time consuming and expensive, and there is no sense inviting trouble. If a shoplifting incident does not strictly meet all three criteria, do not attempt to detain or question a suspected thief. You stand to lose much more than the value of the merchandise the person may be stealing.

In order to be certain that you and your employees know, down to the smallest detail, the proper procedures for detaining a suspected shoplifter, ask the experts for advice. Inquire at your local police station or prosecutor's office, or consult with a private attorney who specializes in criminal matters (a real estate or divorce lawyer, for example, might not be up on all the statutes relating to shoplifting) about the appropriate apprehension guidelines in your area. Make sure that the rules are communicated to all employees, and that every worker agrees to abide by them. The guidelines should also be clearly stated in the store policy manual. There is no sense in risking a lawsuit because someone on your staff wants to be a hero.

Once you are certain that everyone knows the proper procedures for apprehending a shoplifter, the decision must be made as to whether to do so. That decision will be different in every case, depending on the circumstances. If an older person suffering from Alzheimer's disease, who is disoriented and afraid, for example, picks up an item and attempts to leave with it, it would be inappropriate to have that person arrested for shoplifting.

Likewise, if someone is on drugs or displays obviously threatening behavior, it is not worth it for an employee to attempt to detain that person because of the likelihood that the worker will sustain a physical injury. Aside from the fact that it is not sensible for anyone to risk his or her safety in defense of a piece of merchandise, if an employee is injured in this way, the monetary consequences, in the form of workman's compensation payments, and even a possible lawsuit brought by the employee, can spell financial losses for the business far in excess of the cost of the stolen goods.

If an employee feels relatively safe in approaching someone who is shoplifting, there are different ways of handling the incident. If a shoplifter is spotted slipping a book or small item into a bag, a floor employee could approach and say something like, "I think you'll enjoy that book. It's a really good one." Or, "That item also comes in green. Were you looking for any particular color?" An amateur shoplifter will be embarrassed and will probably quickly return the item to the shelf and leave the store. Problem solved.

Another tactic that can be employed if you suspect that someone is stealing is to call the police or your local security force. Speak loudly enough for the thief to hear you. Many shoplifters will leave your store quickly – minus your merchandise – if they think they will be apprehended by law enforcement. This strategy is a non-confrontational way to rid your store of the shoplifter.

If the shoplifter seems to fit the pattern of an experienced thief, you or your employee – whoever has maintained continuous surveillance of the suspected shoplifter – should approach and, speaking calmly and respectfully, identify yourself as a store employee and request that the person go with you to discuss "a matter." Do not say that you would like to discuss a "mistake" or an "oversight" that the person may have made. Using such language could give the shoplifter a legal basis to avoid prosecution. Keep your voice in a normal tone – yelling, threatening, or making accusations can be grounds for the shoplifter to bring a lawsuit against you.

An owner, manager or employee should never attempt to detain a shoplifter alone. It is imperative to have at least one other employee along as a witness to the incident, as well as to observe whether the shoplifter tries to surreptitiously get rid of the merchandise. One of the employees involved should be of the same gender as the suspected shoplifter to avoid sexual misconduct accusations.

When you approach the shoplifter, do not make physical contact – that could also land you in legal hot water. Employees should be clear that they are not to instigate any pushing, shoving or touching of the shoplifter of any sort. Of course, if a shoplifter starts a physical confrontation, employees can defend themselves, but the incident should never be allowed to escalate into a fight. An unstable person could have a weapon and might use it if he or she feels threatened. If the shoplifter wants to get away, don't attempt to stop him or her. Simply memorize his or her description, and try to get information about the vehicle he or she is using – make, model, color, license plate, etc. Turn the description over to the police, and let them pursue the suspect. That's their job.

If the shoplifter does agree to accompany you, lead him or her to a back office or other private area. Have someone call the police right away. Ask the shoplifter to produce a receipt for the merchandise. If he cannot, he will probably tell you a sob story about how this is the first time he's ever done this, or something heartbreaking, like the dying child he's caring for. These stories are almost never true, so don't be lured into feeling guilty. Let the authorities determine whether he's legally culpable for his behavior down the line. He may deny that he has the goods, but if you have followed procedure, you or your employee has kept him and the merchandise in constant view, and you know he has them. Don't try to force the shoplifter to cough up your merchandise on the spot. A better strategy is to let him keep the items concealed, and when law enforcement officers arrive, let them search the suspect and find the goods.

While you're in the office with the shoplifter, request identification. Be aware that any ID or identifying information he gives you may be false. Also keep an eye out for any movement that indicates that he is trying to remove his wallet from his pocket and hide it somewhere to avoid having his real identity known. Write down whatever the person shows you or tells you about his or her identity, especially name and date of birth. Even if it is made-up, it can be used to establish a pattern of dishonest behavior, and the information given may actually be valuable to police in discovering the person's true identity.

Keeping a written record of what the shoplifter tells you is important. You can simplify this task electronically by installing the *Retail Theft Reports Program* (ISBN: 1-889031-42-9) from Looseleaf Law Publications (www.LooseleafLaw.com), which comes on CD-ROM. The program assists you in preparing legally correct reports and automatically generates statements based on the type of incident. Its accounting function also totals the amounts of the stolen items, and the program maintains a searchable database of all apprehensions.

However you prepare your report, you will hand it over to the police when they arrive. The cops will probably ask the suspect for his name and DOB and compare the information to what you wrote down earlier. Within a few minutes, the officers will probably ask the shoplifter for the same information again. If the person is lying, chances are he won't be able to keep the information straight in his head, and something different will come out of his mouth. While he can lie to you without consequence, in many places it is illegal to give a law enforcement officer false identification information, which will add another reason for arrest to the list.

Thieves want to avoid being identified for several reasons. One is that they do not want a criminal record or another charge added to their existing record. If they give a false name, they hope to avoid the consequences of failing to appear in court, fines or other administrative reprimands, which would be issued in the name of a person who doesn't exist. Professional crooks also often dabble in crimes other than shoplifting. There may be arrest warrants issued in their names, and they do not want to go back to jail.

Keep a written record of everything about the incident. Write it down as soon as possible afterwards so that you don't forget anything. You will need to provide the report to the police and to keep it in store records. You will also need it to refresh your memory when the trial finally rolls around – which could be months or years away. Be sure to document everything that you saw, everything that you did, and everything the shoplifter said and did. Be very specific when doing so. Do not say, for example, that the shoplifter "acted in a suspicious manner." Tell exactly what he did that was suspicious. Also include the names and contact information for any witnesses.

A Word About Juveniles

When a shoplifter is a minor, you and your employees must proceed with more caution than when dealing with an adult criminal. Even though they may look grown-up on the outside, minors are still children, and they have rights that adults don't always have. In addition, you need to be certain what local police departments expect of retailers who encounter juvenile shoplifters. In some jurisdictions, the store must notify the police when a juvenile is apprehended; in others, notification depends on parental cooperation. You must consult with the authorities about the proper procedures to employ when apprehending juveniles. This is fertile ground for lawsuits, and store owners can't afford to take that risk.

Dealing with juveniles can be more dangerous than with adults because youths don't realize the consequences of their actions. They may engage in a physical confrontation with store staff or even use a weapon without considering the repercussions.

Young people believe that they are invincible; they are never going to die. They also play video games and watch television and movies with violent content, yet those forms of entertainment don't depict the consequences of violence in an authentic manner. In cartoons, for example, a character is flattened by a car or even killed, only to get up the next moment or to reappear in the next episode. Detective programs show the hero taking a bullet, then going back on the street to solve the case the next day. These incidents aren't realistic, but kids don't always know that. They may copy something they saw on TV, which makes apprehending them riskier than detaining their adult counterparts.

Youths also have different motivations for shoplifting than adults do. Often, they steal on a dare or to be part of the crowd. Very often, the crowd is with them when they make their criminal forays, which means that store staff must keep an eye on several juveniles at the same time. If they are caught, there is a chance that they could develop a "crowd mentality," wherein none of them feel responsibility for what the group does collectively. That adds up to exponentially greater danger for you and your staff when apprehending them.

Depending on your jurisdiction, juveniles are entitled to certain rights, such as having their parents present when they are questioned. Be absolutely certain that you know what is expected of you when detaining a minor, and make sure that your staff is trained to follow procedure to the letter. Again, a criminal attorney, police representative or prosecutor is in the position of advising you what steps are appropriate when a juvenile shoplifts in your store.

The Importance of a Consistent Prosecution Policy

Store owners are often torn about whether to prosecute shoplifters for fear that the report of such an incident will deter customers from shopping there or will tarnish their reputations in the community. Unless you have an excellent reason not to prosecute – such as an elderly person who is taking items out of confusion caused by dementia, for example – you are inviting more theft into your store when you don't bring charges against shoplifters. Thieves hang around with other criminals, and they talk. If your store gets a reputation as an "easy steal," all their friends will come to visit you – and these are not the "customers" you want to attract.

Insofar as discouraging legitimate customers from coming to the store, it is usually not an issue. People know that there are shoplifters in the world, and logic dictates that shoplifters go to stores to steal. By prosecuting them, you will gain a reputation as a good businessperson, and patrons may actually be attracted to your store. They will get the idea that because you are employing good crime-prevention techniques, they will be safe in your establishment. A prominently posted sign that says "We Prosecute Shoplifters to the Fullest Extent of the Law" serves the dual purpose of reassuring legitimate customers and deterring shoplifters. If stronger wording is necessary, a sign that says something like "The Store Reserves the Right to Use Electronic Devices to Detect Shoplifting" or "The Last 250 People Caught Shoplifting Didn't Think Anyone Was Watching Either" might be more effective.

The issue of whether to prosecute a juvenile is a little trickier than when adults are shoplifting. While you do want to discourage thieves from sending their friends to you, many youths aren't professional shoplifters. If they are stealing because of peer pressure to do so "on a dare," for example, the process of being caught, reprimanded and possibly barred from the store in the future may be enough to teach them a lesson. If you prosecute, you will be in the position of giving an otherwise good kid a criminal record. On the other hand, minors can be drug addicts or hardcore thieves, too. If this is the case, your sympathy and failure to throw the book at them will not be helpful to them. In fact, letting such a youth off the hook will teach him that he can continue to commit crimes and get away with them.

Good judgment is called for when deciding what action to take against a minor. If the youth's parents show up and are appropriately concerned and indicate that they will take corrective action, then you may solve the problem by banning the kid from the store. However, if the police are called and the cops seem to know the minor very well from previous scrapes, then you may be dealing with a chronic youthful offender, and prosecution may be the best way to deal with the issue.

It should go without saying that you should not base your judgment on the juvenile's race or socio-economic status. Plenty of poor, minority kids have parents who will not tolerate this sort of behavior – and vice versa. There are many cases of wealthy parents who truly do not care about their children and who will use their money to fix any problems the kids have, just to get them out of their hair. What it ultimately comes down to is whether you believe that the particular juvenile will pose a continued threat to your business if you do not prosecute. You must make the best business decision you can based on the facts at hand. If you should err on the side of leniency, simply banning the youth from the store without prosecuting, and he comes back in and steals again, you can always prosecute at that point.

Once you have made the decision to call the police regarding any shoplifting matter, be sure to tell the cops about any theft patterns you know of elsewhere. Shoplifters sometimes work in rings, hitting a town or an area and stealing electronics, certain types of clothing, or expensive eyeglass frames, for example. Arming the authorities with all the information you have means that you and other merchants have a better chance of hanging onto your stock.

Detection Devices: EAS, CCTV, Mirrors

Certain security devices can help reduce shoplifting, if employees remember that these items are just another tool in the retailer's bag of crime-prevention tricks, not a solution in and of themselves. Staff members must still be alert and customer-service oriented to thwart would-be thieves.

◆ *Electronic Article Surveillance Tags*

Electronic article surveillance, or EAS, tags can be attached to almost any piece of merchandise. Many of them work in conjunction with a shoulder-high device called a pedestal, which is placed just before the exit doors, either alone or in pairs; special floor mats in front of exits; overhead sensors near exit doors; or sensors inside mannequins placed by the exits. (See Figure 4.1.) If an activated EAS tag is not removed, it can trigger some sort of alarm – a beep, flashing lights, bells, etc. – when it passes a pedestal, floor mat, or other sensor. More advanced EAS systems have cameras built into the sensors. When an alarm is triggered, a photograph is automatically taken, thus capturing a thief's image on film.

Other types of EAS tags are designed to make a noise if someone tampers with them. The constant noise encourages thieves to drop the merchandise and leave, rather than taking the source of the noise, which is attached to the stolen item, along with them as they leave the store.

Figure 4.1

Photo courtesy ADT Security Services, Inc.

EAS tags can be placed on merchandise by workers inside the store, or they can be affixed to items by the manufacturer, which is called "source tagging." (See Figure 4.2) Source tagging is convenient for stores that move a lot of small merchandise, such as drug stores. Aspirin bottles, shampoo, suntan lotion and thousands of other items are available to be shipped with EAS tags already on them, thus saving the retailer time and manpower in affixing the tags at the store. The tags often look like bar codes. Naturally, for a store to be able to make use of source tags, it must purchase a pedestal that works with the type of tags the manufacturer uses.

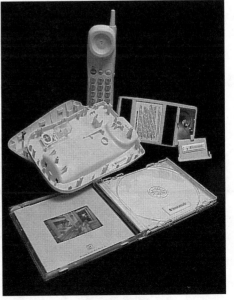

Figure 4.2

Photo courtesy ADT Security Services, Inc.

EAS tags that are affixed to clothing often have a pin device that attaches to the garment and is manually removed by the cashier with a special detacher. (See Figure 4.3.) They are available in large sizes, which are meant to be obvious and are therefore shoplifting deterrents, and in smaller, discreet tags, which are often used in more upscale retail environments. These EAS tags operate on a microwave system, which triggers the alarm when it is in the vicinity of the sensor.

The store owner who chooses to employ EAS pin-type tags to protect merchandise has to purchase the tags as well as the sensors from a security supplier. The sensors generally will work only with the supplier's tags, so systems cannot be switched without incurring the cost of installing an entire new one.

While pin tags can provide protection against loss, the holes they make have been known to ruin clothing. In addition, should a cashier forget to remove a tag, legitimate customers may be inconvenienced and embarrassed when the alarm is triggered as they are leaving the store with their purchases. Dishonest employees or retail-workers-turned-thieves may acquire the know-how to remove the tags without employing the detacher and can defeat the system in that manner, or they can conceal merchandise in a foil-lined "booster bag," which allows them to pass the pedestal without triggering the alarm.

Figure 4.3
Photo courtesy ADT Security Services, Inc.

One strategy that can be employed is to use two tags on clothing – a regular pin tag that is affixed in a prominent place on the garment, as well as a smaller, hidden one. Expert thieves or dishonest employees may remove the obvious tag and, believing that it is safe to bypass the pedestal without triggering the alarm, attempt to leave the store, unaware that the hidden tag will activate the alarm.

Another type of EAS tag works on a radio frequency (RF). These tags are designed to set off an alarm when they pass by sensors. RF tags have the advantage of being deactivated by store personnel more easily than bulky pin tags. The deactivation function can be combined with a price scanning function in the same device, eliminating the need for a separate deactivator. Because these tags work on a radio frequency that covers a certain field, the cashier does not have to physically make contact with the tag in order to deactivate it – a real time-saver. RF EAS tags also tend to be less costly than the pin-tag types. Another advantage of these tags is that they can be set up to work with different radio frequencies. In a large store with many departments, the frequencies can be set so that customers can carry items from one department to another without setting off an alarm until reaching the exit-door sensors.

Magnetic EAS tags are a third option for retailers. Many people are familiar with this system because it is the same type that is used in libraries. Sensors emit a magnetic field that detects tags or labels containing magnetic material, which are affixed to the merchandise. The cashier (or librarian) deactivates the tags or labels by passing the item over a magnetic pad.

This system has a few drawbacks. One is that many devices today depend in some part on magnetic technology. The system can interfere with computers, software, price scanning equipment, credit cards with magnetic strips, and so forth, which also makes them impractical for stores that sell electronic items. Another is that foreign metal objects can trigger the alarm when they pass by the sensors, which can result in customer inconvenience and embarrassment, especially when they have no store merchandise in their possession.

Regardless of which type of EAS system is in place, detachers and deactivators should be kept well behind the counter, out of reach of customers who may attempt to remove the tags themselves without making a purchase.

◆ *Closed Circuit TV*

Closed-circuit television (CCTV) systems are effective theft deterrents. Shoplifters want to remain anonymous, and they cannot do so if
a CCTV camera captures the image of them as they are committing a
theft. Stores with CCTV systems are also less likely to be targeted by
burglars for the same reason.

Figure 4.4
Photo courtesy ADT Security Services, Inc.

Cameras can be mounted on the walls and ceilings and can be visible
or hidden within a dark-colored dome. Cameras can be set to run
continuously, recording the goings-on of the store and displaying the
images in real-time on monitors in the security office of a large store, or
simply recording them in time-lapse fashion. (See Figure 4.4.) More
sophisticated cameras can pan, tilt and zoom in on particular areas that
a security officer wants to see in more detail at any given time, such as
a furtive customer or a suspected dishonest employee. The images
recorded by one camera at a time, or several cameras simultaneously,
can be projected onto one monitor screen, or onto a number of monitors,
depending on the size of the store.

In a smaller store, theft deterrence through the use of CCTV can be
achieved by displaying the images on a monitor that is visible to employees and customers alike.

In an establishment where discretion is important – or when an
investigation is underway – covert camera systems can be employed.

Sometimes termed "nanny-cams" for their popularity among parents who want to clandestinely monitor their children's caretakers in their homes, these small cameras can be placed virtually anywhere. About the size of a credit card, the miniature devices, which are hidden inside dolls, clocks, mannequins, or any number of other places, record and transmit images to a monitor.

CCTV cameras can also be hooked up to detection devices for after-hours surveillance. When a motion sensor is triggered, the system begins recording and simultaneously dials a programmed telephone number and transmits images over the telephone lines to a designated off-premises monitor. In this way, alarm companies or store owners can get a look at exactly what's happening inside the store. This type of system can also be linked to EAS systems to record any movement in the area of the EAS device that is triggered.

CCTV technology can become costly, depending on the size of the retail area that must be protected and the bells and whistles that are part of the system an owner selects. If theft deterrence is the only object and the budget to accomplish it is minuscule, that goal can be accomplished in some measure through the use of fake cameras and/or domes. The cameras or domes are affixed to the walls or ceilings where the real McCoys would be placed. Potential shoplifters who think that the premises are under surveillance might seek greener, unprotected pastures elsewhere.

The key to being successful with these fake contraptions is to purchase cameras that look real. A camera that resembles a kid's toy will fool no one and may increase thefts when the word circulates around the criminal community that the store is not employing detection devices. Many pretend cameras on the market look real and have wires that extend to plates meant to be attached to the wall. Some of them even swivel at intervals, as though someone were monitoring the store and moving the camera around to get a good look.

◆ *Mirrors*

Wide-angle mirrors can be placed in strategic locations to make it easier for employees to see what's going on in places that they would otherwise not have visual access to, such as around corners, over partitions, or in remote areas of the store. These mirrors work the same way for shoplifters, however, who can likewise keep an eye on store staff.

One-way mirrors reflect an image to the person looking at the glass on one side, but allow someone on the other side of the pane to see through to the other side. These can be positioned inside ceiling domes and monitored by security personnel who can communicate with other security officers stationed on the floor using walkie-talkies or radios. They can also be placed in inner offices, either to monitor the activities of employees in a cash room, or to allow store personnel a view of the sales floor.

Fitting-Room Risks

Clothing try-on rooms represent an area of significant opportunity for theft. If fitting rooms are short-staffed, the store is vulnerable to losses in several ways. Shoplifters will take advantage of the lack of personnel to conceal and make off with extra garments, and sales to legitimate customers will be lost if there is no one available to assist them. The key to reducing fitting-room losses is to ensure that enough employees are assigned to the area to provide excellent customer service, which is a theft deterrent in itself, as well as to avoid leaving the area unattended.

When no employees are posted at the entrance to the try-on area, there is no way to monitor how many garments customers bring in versus how many they leave with. A properly trained fitting room attendant has the customer hand her the clothing upon entering. The attendant should then count and shake out each piece individually, explaining that new garments are often stiff, and she is loosening them up for the customer. If a customer with dishonest intentions has concealed one garment inside another, shaking the clothing out will reveal that fact.

Tags that are labeled with digits that correspond to the number of pieces a customer brings in should be presented, and the fitting room attendant should show the customer to an empty try-on room and hang the garments and tag inside for her. It's best to limit the number of pieces of clothing allowed inside a fitting room at one time to between four and six. The salesperson can put the rest of the clothing on a designated rack and assure the customer that she will bring her additional pieces when she is ready to exchange the ones she has already tried on for the new ones. In this way, the staff can control the number of pieces a customer has at any one time.

Almost nothing is more frustrating to a shopper who is standing in her underwear than to find that there is no salesperson available to help her find alternative items. Sales to legitimate customers will be lost if they have to keep leaving the fitting room to search for other sizes or colors. At some point – probably sooner rather than later – a customer will get dressed in her own clothes and leave without buying anything, and the likelihood that she will return is slim.

Solicitous salespeople will keep checking on customers in the fitting rooms, offering to fetch them bigger or smaller sizes or alternative colors, and bringing them accessories such as belts, socks or hats that will complement an outfit. In this way, customers feel cared about and are likely to make a purchase and to return to the store, sales increase, and the opportunity for theft is diminished.

When the customer exits the fitting room, the attendant should compare the number of garments she has with her to the number on the tag to ensure that they match, then escort the customer to the cashier, carrying the clothing for her. As soon as a shopper vacates a try-on room, staff members should check it, looking for personal belongings that the customer may have forgotten, or stray hangers or a garment, which might indicate that the customer has concealed an item or has put on the store's clothing, leaving her old clothes behind.

Prevention Strategies: Locking Cases, Benefit-Denial Tags, Cable-Locks, the Hanger Trick

As opposed to devices designed to detect shoplifting, prevention strategies are employed to eliminate the opportunities for theft. As with any merchandising decision, each loss prevention method must take into account the potential inconvenience to the legitimate customer, along with the value of the items being protected. It makes no sense, for example, to invest huge sums of money in elaborate loss prevention equipment to protect low-dollar-value goods. It is also counter-productive to secure every product in the store, yet not have sufficient personnel available to unlock cabinets or cables. But by using a balanced approach, locking cases, benefit-denial tags, cable-locks and proper hanger arrangement can be effective theft deterrents without sacrificing sales.

◆ *Locking Cases*

An attractive display case or cabinet can be a sales asset as well as a protective device when used to house high-dollar items, such as jewelry or electronics. Locking cases should allow customers easy observation of merchandise to encourage sales, and attractive displays can be set up inside the case in order to attract attention. As long as workers are available to unlock and show the items, the cases should not inhibit sales.

Locks should be positioned so that customers cannot reach around or over the case and unlock it themselves. Salespeople must be trained to limit the number of items they bring at one time, and to lock the cabinet after replacing the items and finishing with each customer. It is a good idea to provide staff members with key holders that are worn around the neck or the wrist, rather than designating a place to keep the keys, where customers could easily get unauthorized access to them.

Some custom cabinet designers have developed ingenious display racks or cases that provide product protection while giving the illusion that the merchandise is accessible. There are sunglass racks, for example, that display the eye wear in vertical rows, each pair nestled on an inverted V. Customers can touch the glasses, but they cannot remove them without having a salesperson release them, either individually or in a group, depending on the display model.

◆ *Benefit-Denial Tags*

Somewhat similar in appearance to an EAS tag is the "benefit-denial tag," which is designed to deny the shoplifter the benefit of using or wearing stolen goods. If thieves abscond with merchandise to which this type of device is affixed, the item becomes useless to them once they attempt to remove the tag. Clothing benefit-denial tags are designed to emit a beep as well as to squirt ink on the garment – and on the thief's hands – when it is removed without using the offi-

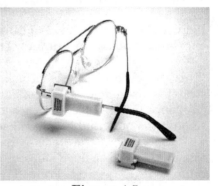

Figure 4.5
Photo courtesy ADT Security Services, Inc.

cial detaching equipment. Other benefit-denial tags are designed for smaller items, such as jewelry or sunglasses. (See Figure 4.5) In that case, when the shoplifter tries to remove the tag, the item breaks, thus robbing the thief of the ability to wear or resell the item.

It seems counter-intuitive to allow a thief to make off with the store's merchandise only to ruin the item long after the shoplifter is off the premises. However, as fast as security devices are created and put on the market, thieves become aware of them. Unless a shoplifter is a rank amateur, he will recognize the benefit-denial tag and bypass that item or that store, knowing that he will not be able to enjoy the fruits of his labors. An amateur who is unpleasantly surprised by the benefit-denial tag will probably give up his or her burgeoning life of crime at that point, and will no longer pose a threat to the store.

◆   *Cable-Locks*

A cable-locking system is used to anchor merchandise to a central point so that thieves cannot pick it up and walk off with it, or to set off an alarm if someone tampers with the product to which the lock is attached. Some cable-locks are designed so that customers can handle or try merchandise on but cannot remove it from the immediate area without a salesperson's assistance. Different types of cable-locks can be used on larger, high-dollar merchandise, such as leather or fur coats; on smaller goods, such as shoes, belts or pocketbooks; and on hard goods, such as electronics and power tools.

Garment cable-locks often have a ball-and-loop system that is linked through the sleeve or other area of the clothing item and connect to a central lock box. Systems for smaller products include lanyards connected to anti-theft tags, while larger, hard goods can be protected using electronic cables that trigger an alarm if they are removed from the merchandise.

While cable-locks are sometimes frustrating for the customer who wants to handle or try on merchandise, as with other loss-prevention strategies, good customer service is the solution to eliminating the annoyance of limited access while increasing sales of high-dollar items.

◆   *The Hanger Trick*

Clothing stores can reduce mass shoplifting attempts for no cost at all, simply by changing the way the garments are placed on racks. By arranging hangers in alternating directions – one hanger faces inward, the next faces outward, the next inward, the next outward, and so on – thieves will be frustrated if they attempt to grab a handful of clothes at one time and run off with them. Legitimate customers won't be inconvenienced because the direction that the hanger faces doesn't affect the shopper's ability to slide it down the rack and examine the next item. Customers who want to remove a garment generally select one piece at a time, and it's easy for them to see which way they need to slide the hanger to take the clothing off the rack.

Recognizing Booster Bags and Boxes

A "booster bag" or "booster box" is a container that shoplifters use to conceal items they are stealing, or "boosting." A booster bag or box is often a converted shopping bag or box that sports the name and logo of a legitimate store, or is wrapped to look like a gift.

Booster bags can be lined with aluminum foil or another metal in order to prevent sensors from detecting the presence of an activated EAS tag as the shoplifter removes stolen items from the store. Booster boxes are sometimes fitted with a false bottom or a spring device so that when the box is set on top of or next to a desired piece of merchandise, the item is "swallowed" by the box.

One tip-off that a patron may be employing a booster bag or booster box is if the bag or box comes from a store that is not in your shopping or strip mall, or that you don't recognize as being a local business. Legitimate shoppers don't carry bulky bags and boxes around with them. They generally leave their purchases in their cars when they go to the next store. Good customer service is the key. Invite shoppers to leave their packages at the customer service desk as they enter the store. If they decline or leave the store rather than checking their bags, they may have entered with the intent to steal.

Other devices used to conceal merchandise include baby carriages, which can be modified to include a large empty area underneath the baby's mattress where products can be stashed. Often, there is no baby in the carriage, or the "infant" is really a doll.

"Booster coats" are fitted out with many pockets and hooks the wearer can use to conceal merchandise. (Remember the example of the person who doesn't fit in because he enters the store wearing an overcoat in July? It is likely a shoplifter in a booster coat.) "Booster bloomers" consist of a pant-like garment that is worn under loose clothing and that ties around each leg, providing a large pocket into which clothing and other goods can be concealed. Similarly, professional shoplifters, or "crotch carriers" can perform what is known as the "crotch walk," which consists of concealing merchandise between the thighs and under a long dress or coat, and walking out with it. Amazingly, proficient thieves can walk off with very heavy, bulky items in this manner.

There is no limit to the devices that crafty shoplifters will think up to separate stores from their merchandise. Having eagle-eyed floor personnel who provide excellent customer service is still the best way to overcome any ingenious plot cooked up by thieves.

Combating Theft Rings: The Telephone Tree

Although shoplifting is sometimes a random act, it can also be part of a pattern of thefts in your local area or region. If your store does get hit, it is in your best interest to warn other merchants. Naturally, unless there is an apprehension and arrest, you don't want to accuse anyone based on personal suspicion of wrongdoing (that could lead to a slander lawsuit). But letting your colleagues know about theft patterns is not only the neighborly thing to do, it will lead to greater protection for the entire community.

If your store is hit by an individual or a gang of thieves, a quick way to circulate word to other retailers is via a "telephone tree." Immediately after the theft, you call two shopkeepers, then they call two, and so on. Especially if the thieves are targeting a particular item or type of merchandise (eyeglass frames, VCRs, jewelry, or what have you), stores can have their personnel keep a particularly close eye on those products. If the shoplifters are making the rounds, serially ripping off stores, spreading the word around town quickly can thwart their efforts.

As an alternative to the telephone tree, each retailer can have an e-mail list in place and shoot out the shoplifters' descriptions and any other information as soon as it is known. The drawback to using e-mail for this kind of notification is that unless the recipients check their e-mail constantly, they may not get the word until it's too late. Also, people frequently change their e-mail addresses, and an electronic message may never get to the intended party; whereas, if you communicate via telephone, you can immediately impart the pertinent information to whoever answers.

Work out the best form of communication for your circumstances at the next council or association meeting, or wherever local retailers get together in your area. If there is no regular meeting, then take the initiative to form a telephone tree by calling a couple of retailers and getting them on board. They can call a few more, and so on. It is a small investment in time for a large pay-off.

Chapter 5
CHECK IT OUT

Although electronic transactions are gaining popularity, many customers still prefer to pay by check. While there is some risk involved in accepting checks, statistics show that in many instances, the cost of accepting checks can actually work out to be less than the cost of accepting cash, when such tasks as counting, safeguarding, preparing reports and transporting the cash or checks for deposit are factored in. In fact, some businesses do not accept cash as payment in order to reduce the risk of robbery.

Regardless of merchant preferences, retail businesses will probably have to accept checks for the foreseeable future in order to remain competitive. Most retailers allow their customers to pay either by credit card or by check. Some customers would rather write checks because they don't want to incur interest charges on their charge accounts or because they can use checks to keep better track of their cash flow. According to the Washington, D.C.-based Check Payment Systems Association, 42.5 billion checks were written in the United States in 2000, which accounted for nearly $40 trillion. In the retail arena, checks represent almost 60 percent of non-cash retail transactions, often because consumers prefer to write checks to pay for larger transactions – the average consumer check is estimated at $364.

Years ago, merchants often accepted third-party checks or cashed payroll checks for their customers. This practice is no longer a good idea. For one thing, it places the store in the position of acting like a bank. Even if the check is perfectly good and clears without any problems, the store has paid out funds that will not be recouped until the bank releases the funds into the business' account. For another, if the check doesn't clear, getting payment for a third-party check can be a difficult, drawn-out process – and even then, the money might not be recovered. In addition, check fraud has increased, and it is hard to verify that a payroll check that appears to be issued by a large company is the real thing – or a computer-generated fake. Also, a government pension or Social Security check may be legitimate – but stolen from the real recipient's mailbox and presented in your store. It's best to steer customers to a bank or local check-cashing office, rather than taking on the responsibility of cashing a check or accepting a third-party check.

Most people don't give any thought to what a check actually is and isn't. It *isn't* money; a check is simply a written promise to transfer funds from the writer's bank account to yours. To make sure that checks will be paid by the bank on which they are drawn, the check has to be filled out properly, and the person accepting the check has to follow established acceptance protocol. By ensuring that all employees carefully follow procedures, use good common sense, and get a supervisor's or manager's approval for each check, your chances of being ripped off by a bad-check writer will fall dramatically.

Technology: the Pros and Cons

Check-writing scams that affect retailers have increased in the last few years. Checks are so commonplace that most people don't examine them carefully. The scant attention that is paid to checks, coupled with the fact that advanced technology is so readily available, means that bad checks are often accepted by stores.

The proliferation of desktop publishing and laser scanners and printers has made it easier for criminals to forge, duplicate and print fraudulent checks. The equipment is so readily available that anyone with access to a library or a store that makes computer equipment available at an hourly rate can print out a check that looks good at first glance. The increased access to technology means that it isn't only career criminals who have the wherewithal to create counterfeit checks. Today, anyone from the college kid next door to your grandmother has the same opportunity to commit these crimes.

The upside of technological advances is that check manufacturers also have access to them. Security-minded check printers have developed a number of features that are incorporated into the checks themselves to make it easier for retailers to distinguish legitimate checks from bad paper.

One way to determine whether you have a real check, as opposed to a computer-generated fake, is to look for the Check Payment Systems Association's padlock icon, which usually appears to the right of the written dollar amount line, and which is the recognized symbol for fraud-evident protections in paper checks. The CPSA padlock icon indicates that a legitimately printed check incorporates at least three security features. (See Figure 5.1) If the icon is present, but you don't see the security features, the check may be a fake.

The minimum number of security features required for use of the icon at (3).

Icon with warning verbiage on check front combined with.....

Warning box back constitutes one (educational) feature.

Figure 5.1

One security feature includes the padlock icon coupled with a warning statement, such as "Security features are included. Details on back." Along with the icon and statement, the back of the check has a box, also identified with the padlock icon, and a list of the security features of that particular check. (See Figure 5.2) When the padlock icon appears, the check must also contain at least one anti-alteration feature, such as chemically sensitive paper, which shows stains or spots if

This standard also incorporates ideas for improved warning box backs to better educate both the recipient and the presenter on how to authenticate a check or detect alteration.

Figure 5.2

Courtesy Check Payment Systems Assn.

someone tries to alter the check chemically (See Figure 5.3), plus one anti-counterfeiting feature, such as the letters "MP," which may appear to the right of the signature line (See Figure 5.4). The MP mark indicates that the signature line is not actually solid, but is microprinted with words such as "Authorized Signature." The microprinting can be spotted using a strong magnifying glass, and it cannot be duplicated with a desktop computer system.

Multistain Security Paper

Figure 5.3

Courtesy Check Payment Systems Assn.

Other security features that accompany the padlock include some sort of security screen on the back side of the check, featuring the words "Original Document" or the printer's brand name, plus a security weave pattern. If there is none, or if the word "Void" appears near the statement on the back side, that is an indication that the check is counterfeit. Also, if a pattern of blue and green fibers are sprinkled throughout the check paper, they will be invisible to the naked eye but will be revealed by holding the check under ultraviolet light. (See Figure 5.5) Another safety feature is designed to make alterations obvious if someone should attempt to erase anything written in ink, such as the dollar amount, payee name, or signature.

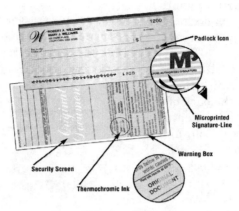

Figure 5.4

Ultraviolet Feature:

An invisible, random pattern of blue and green fibers appears on your check when held to an ultraviolet light source.

Figure 5.5

Courtesy Check Payment Systems Assn.

Even if the check you are presented with is a cashier's check or a bank check, it is possible that it is a fake. If you suspect that this kind of check isn't real, call the bank that issued it and ask for verification.

Close Scrutiny

Verifying that the check itself is real is an important step, but it is just the first. It is crucial to establish that the customer is who he or she purports to be. To do so, get at least two forms of identification from the check writer, including at least one with a photo. State- or government-issued photo IDs, such as passports, driver's licenses, or military ID cards, are best (as opposed to unofficial identification cards that can be made up in any photo shop). Keep in mind that U.S. government policy dictates that Social Security cards are never acceptable as identification. Also remember that you cannot record on the check the account numbers of credit cards that are presented for identification purposes.

Write the pertinent information, such as the ID card number, on the back of the check, and compare the name, address, signature and other details to those on the face of the check. Also, pay attention when taking down the customer's home and work telephone numbers – some slick check writers will give you a commonly known number, such as for the time or weather service, instead of their own.

It is a good idea to post your store's check-acceptance policy at the register. Some of the requirements that make sense, aside from customer I.D., include the refusal to accept "starter" checks or checks that do not have an address printed on them along with the account-holder's name. Starter checks are the ones given to the account-holder by the bank to be used temporarily until the printed checks arrive. They typically have low check numbers – usually under 100. Regular checks can be ordered without a name or an address printed on them. If there is no name or address on the check, then the cashier will have nothing to compare to the information on the customer's I.D. Therefore, the potential for fraud increases. "Counter checks" are another type of check that would not have a printed name or address. These checks are given by the bank to the account-holder to use. Counter checks are usually requested by customers who have run out of checks and just need one or a few to tide them over until the printed checks arrive. These checks often have very high check numbers, sometimes seven digits long. Again, slick crooks could use them to defraud merchants.

There are a lot of things to pay attention to on the check itself. Some of the most obvious clues to a check that might not be paid are often the ones that are most overlooked by busy shopkeepers:

♦ If a check appears with mysterious marks, blots or erasures, beware! These spots could indicate more than a sloppy customer – they could be telling you that the person presenting the check is not the account holder.
♦ Make sure the date is today's. Don't accept a check if it is post-dated or stale-dated (over six months old).
♦ Look at the numeric value of the check as well as the amount written out on the dollar line. The two need to match.
♦ The transit number on the bottom left or middle of each check is always nine digits long and surrounded by a stop symbol: an upright dash followed by two dots. If the number is not nine digits long, or if it is not surrounded by a stop code, it is not a valid check.
♦ The check needs to be made out properly to your business name. If it is made out to another party, you won't be able to cash it.

◆ Look at the signature on the IDs and on the check – do they match? If not, or if there seems to be something a little "off" about the signature, the check or the transaction in general, refuse (nicely) to take the check and request another form of payment.

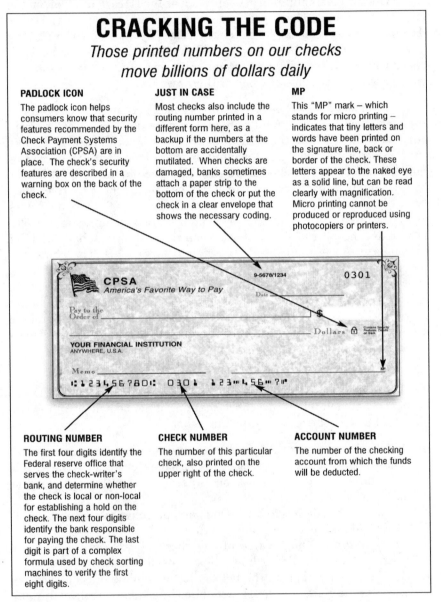

CRACKING THE CODE
Those printed numbers on our checks
move billions of dollars daily

PADLOCK ICON

The padlock icon helps consumers know that security features recommended by the Check Payment Systems Association (CPSA) are in place. The check's security features are described in a warning box on the back of the check.

JUST IN CASE

Most checks also include the routing number printed in a different form here, as a backup if the numbers at the bottom are accidentally mutilated. When checks are damaged, banks sometimes attach a paper strip to the bottom of the check or put the check in a clear envelope that shows the necessary coding.

MP

This "MP" mark – which stands for micro printing – indicates that tiny letters and words have been printed on the signature line, back or border of the check. These letters appear to the naked eye as a solid line, but can be read clearly with magnification. Micro printing cannot be produced or reproduced using photocopiers or printers.

ROUTING NUMBER

The first four digits identify the Federal reserve office that serves the check-writer's bank, and determine whether the check is local or non-local for establishing a hold on the check. The next four digits identify the bank responsible for paying the check. The last digit is part of a complex formula used by check sorting machines to verify the first eight digits.

CHECK NUMBER

The number of this particular check, also printed on the upper right of the check.

ACCOUNT NUMBER

The number of the checking account from which the funds will be deducted.

Figure 5.6

Travelers Checks

Another possibility for suffering a loss involves travelers checks. Travelers checks are issued by companies such as American Express, VISA, MasterCard and Citicorp, and are often used by travelers who don't want to carry a lot of cash around. They are made out to a payee, just like a regular check, and signed by the buyer when they are purchased. A second signature blank appears, where the buyer is to countersign at the time of purchase. The signatures must match in order for the travelers check to be paid by the issuing company.

When criminals pull a scam with travelers checks, they will often use a large denomination check to pay for small purchases. One-hundred-dollar checks are a popular amount. The thief gets the low-cost item, plus the real cash that the store gives as change for the fake travelers check.

Forgers can practice someone else's signature until they get it right, especially if they have an example right on the same document. To be sure that the right person is presenting the travelers check, make sure the customer signs the check in front of you. Don't accept it if it is presented with both signatures already on it. Check the signature against a legitimate ID, and compare it to the ones on the check. Use common sense, and if you have a bad feeling about the transaction, "Just say no."

Counterfeit travelers checks can also be made on laser printers or color copiers. To spot the differences between a legitimate travelers check and a fake, look for engraved or embossed printing, and check out the paper quality. Travelers checks have a raised texture and the crisp feel of currency. Some also include a watermark, hologram, and at least three distinct ink colors. (See Figure 5.7) These features cannot be duplicated using desktop publishing equipment. In addition, some travelers checks have an additional security feature that makes the word "Void" visible if the check is photocopied.

If you have suspicions about the authenticity of a travelers check, you can always call the issuing company and give them the unique serial number of the check. You can also fax a copy of the check to them. The issuing company can verify whether the serial number is one that has been sold and can look at the faxed copy of the check to determine whether it is a forgery.

The policies about honoring a bad travelers check vary by company. American Express, which is well known for its travelers checks, for example, will pay a merchant who has accepted a counterfeit check as long as the check isn't a blatantly obvious fake, and as long as the cashier watches the customer countersign the check.

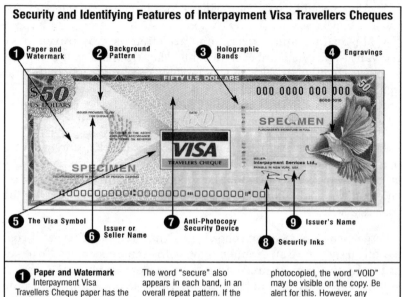

Security and Identifying Features of Interpayment Visa Travellers Cheques

1 Paper and Watermark
2 Background Pattern
3 Holographic Bands
4 Engravings
5 The Visa Symbol
6 Issuer or Seller Name
7 Anti-Photocopy Security Device
8 Security Inks
9 Issuer's Name

Figure 5.7

① Paper and Watermark Interpayment Visa Travellers Cheque paper has the crisp feel of currency. When a cheque is held up to the light, a watermark of the Visa Dove can be seen in the blank area to the left. If this watermark is not clearly visible, the cheque may be a counterfeit. When in doubt, please phone our 24-hour customer service centre.

② Background Pattern The background is multicoloured and multi-patterned. A blue pattern on the right side of the cheque blends into pink toward the centre. The word "VISA", followed by the cheque currency and denomination, are rendered in yellow-tan and grey rays.

③ Holographic Bands Silver, metallic, holographic bands appear to the right of the Visa Symbol. When the cheque is tilted, the colours within the bands will appear to change.

The word "secure" also appears in each band, in an overall repeat pattern. If the colour of the bands appears black, the cheque may be a counterfeit.

④ Engravings Engraving is used on the Visa Dove, the cheque's border, and the Primary Denomination Indicator in the upper left corner. These engravings have a slightly raised texture, and the printing is sharp and clear, not blurred.

⑤ The Visa Symbol The blue, white and gold Visa Symbol is prominently displayed on all Interpayment Visa Travellers Cheques.

⑥ Issuer or Seller Name The issuer's name, or that of a sales agent, may appear here, or the area may be blank.

⑦ Anti-photocopy Security Feature If an Interpayment Visa Travellers Cheque is

photocopied, the word "VOID" may be visible on the copy. Be alert for this. However, any photocopy will also lack other security features described here.

⑧ Security Inks If alterations to the purchaser's signature have been made, the background pattern in the signature area may be smudged or erased and some discolouration may also be evident.

⑨ Issuer's Name The name of the cheque issuer will always appear in this area.

NOTE: Some Interpayment Visa Travellers Cheques may carry instructions for encashment or negotiation. These will appear on the cheque's reverse side.

To avoid hassles with your bank, it is a good idea to accept travelers checks that are drawn on U.S. currency only. Until U.S. banks become friendlier toward foreign currency, you will need to consider whether it is worth your while to take foreign travelers checks. If the check is issued in foreign currency, you may have to pay a funds collection fee and/or wait a long time before your bank releases the money to you. In addition, if you accept foreign currency or travelers checks, you will have to figure out the exchange rate, which may be different when you deposit the check than when you take it in, thereby effectively altering the amount of money that you have received from the customer. Your bank can explain the fees and time frames that apply to foreign currency deposits into business accounts. If you are in an area that draws a lot of visitors from overseas, it is a good idea to educate yourself about these issues before a customer comes in and puts you on the spot.

Government Checks

If you do choose to accept U.S. government checks in your store, there are certain security features that will help you distinguish a real one from a counterfeit.

According to the U.S. Secret Service, the paper used for Treasury checks is chemically responsive to solvents and ink removers that make most alterations easy to notice. It also contains a continuous pattern watermark that says "U.S. Treasury." This security feature cannot be reproduced using a typical photocopier.

In addition, the inks that are used in the printing process are designed to react to leaching and bleaching, so that they fade when rubbed with water and dissolve when exposed to alcohol or bleach, which makes most attempted alterations noticeable. The ink colors are also difficult to reproduce on most photocopiers. The Treasury Seal is printed with a bleeding ink that will smudge red when it is exposed to moisture.

According to the U.S. Secret Service, the paper used for Treasury checks is chemically responsive to solvents and ink removers that make most alterations easy to notice. It also contains a continuous pattern watermark that says "U.S. Treasury." This security feature cannot be reproduced using a typical photocopier.

In addition, the inks that are used in the printing process are designed to react to leaching and bleaching, so that they fade when rubbed with water and dissolve when exposed to alcohol or bleach, which makes most attempted alterations noticeable. The ink colors are also difficult to reproduce on most photocopiers. The Treasury Seal is printed with a bleeding ink that will smudge red when it is exposed to moisture.

The signature line on the back of the check is comprised of micro-printed text that repeats the letters "USA." The checks also have a fluorescent image printed in the centers. It can be viewed under ultraviolet light, but cannot be reproduced by most photocopiers.

Government checks are never issued with corrections. If there are any present, it is a sign that the check has been altered. As with any other type of check, be on the lookout for erasures, strikeovers, or pen-and-ink corrections; bleaching or other color changes around letters or numbers; or uneven spacing or misalignment of type.

Use common sense when considering whether a government check is legitimate. It is unlikely that a Social Security check, for example, would be issued for thousands of dollars, so compare the amount of the check with the reason for which it was drawn.

If someone attempts to give you a government check that you suspect may be counterfeit or altered, alert local law enforcement or the U.S. Secret Service.

Money Orders

A customer might pay with a money order when ordering by mail, but it is unlikely that someone would present a money order for an on-the-spot purchase. Money orders are issued in specific amounts requested by the purchaser. Unless the customer has come in before-hand to learn the total cost of a specific item, it would be hard for him to have a money order already prepared in the exact amount due.

Should you have reason to accept money orders, you should be familiar with the appearance of a legitimate one. A lot of money orders are purchased from the post office; however, there are many other companies and banks that also issue their own money orders. Each one will look different, depending on who the issuer is. If you have any questions about the authenticity of a money order, contact the issuing institution before releasing the merchandise.

A Postal Money Order is often considered to be the safest type of money order to accept because of its recognizable appearance and safety design. Look for these features by holding the money order up to the light:

◆ **Watermark.** A watermark of Benjamin Franklin appears in the gray oval on the left-hand side of the front of the money order.
◆ **Security thread.** A security thread runs vertically down the money order approximately one-third of the way from the left edge. The letters "USPS" are repeated in very small letters in the security thread. If there is a dark strip where the security thread belongs,

but there are no small letters within it, it is a sign of a counterfeit money order.

◆ **United States Postal Service shield.** The USPS shield appears on the right side of the front of the money order.

◆ **Red lettering on front:** Toward the right-hand side of the front of the money order, the words "See Reverse Warning" appear in red ink.

◆ **Red lettering on back:** The words "Hold to light and check for Benjamin Franklin watermark and security thread" appear in red ink on the back of the money order, about a third of the way down.

◆ **Maximum value.** Postal Money Orders are issued only for dollar amounts up to $1,000.

You should be aware that Postal Money Orders can never be stale-dated. Regardless of when they are issued, they never expire. They can be cashed at any bank or post office.

The USPS publishes a "Missing USPS Money Orders" list. You can check the number of a money order that you receive against the numbers of the missing ones. The "Hot List" has the most recent additions of missing money order numbers. You can access these lists from the USPS Web site at www.usps.com.

If you do take in a money order that you suspect may be counterfeit, try to delay the person who presents it until the authorities arrive. If that's not possible or safe, memorize his or her description, plus that of any vehicle used. Contact your local police or the United States Postal Inspection Service. Limit handling of the money order, and protect it in an envelope or other covering. Turn the suspected counterfeit over only to a law enforcement officer who presents genuine identification. If you're in doubt about whether the person is a real officer, look up the number of the agency that the person says he or she represents, and call for verification.

If you receive a suspect money order by mail, save it and the envelope that it came in, in a protective covering such as a large envelope. Gather all information and paperwork you have regarding the customer and the order, and contact the nearest U.S. Postal Inspection Service office. You can get the telephone number from the information operator, from the phone book, or online at www.usps.com/ncsc/locators/find-is.html. In addition to a counterfeiting charge, the person who sends you the bogus money order can also be prosecuted on mail fraud charges. You will probably be asked to fill out a Form 8165, Mail Fraud Report. If you have Internet access, you can download one at www.usps.com/postalinspectors/ps8165.pdf before the authorities arrive and have it ready for them.

Protect Yourself

There are some circumstances under which the decision to accept a check must be weighed against the inconvenience factor should something go wrong. Checks can be returned to the store unpaid by the banks on which they are drawn for several reasons: the account has been closed or is non-existent; someone impersonating the account owner passed the check; the account holder has instructed the bank not to pay the check; or there is not enough money in the account to pay the check. In addition, keep in mind that it is often difficult to collect on an out-of-state returned check. As far as collecting on a bad check drawn on a foreign bank, you can pretty much forget ever getting that money if the check doesn't clear.

If you are suspicious about the authenticity of a check or an account, you can call the bank to verify that the funds are available. However, in the interest of customer privacy, many banks are moving toward not revealing that information. If the bank does verify checks, remember that the bank can tell you only that the funds are in the account *at that moment*. If the bank confirms that the funds are there but the check writer has made a mathematical error or something else goes wrong, by the time the check hits his or her account, the money may no longer be available to pay the check written to your store.

If you don't have a good feeling about the transaction and the customer has presented a credit card for identification but wants to pay by check, request that you charge the transaction instead. Point out that if the customer immediately sends the check to his credit card company to pay for the transaction, he will not incur any interest fees.

If you want to discourage someone from paying by check without insulting him, take him to the side and have him fill out a "Good Customer Form," or whatever you choose to call it. Explain that you will put down all the necessary information about the person, such as name, address, telephone, proof of identity, bank information, and so on, and keep it on file. If the check-writer wants to write checks in the future, all that information will be there, so the process will go more quickly next time. You can also say that your store will send notices of special sales that are available only to people in the "Good Customer File." If someone wants to pass bad paper, this scrutiny will send them packing. On the other hand, legitimate customers will appreciate the fact that they have to go through this procedure only once – and who wouldn't want to get in on a special sale?

You can also cut your risks by subscribing to a check verification service. Although there are fees involved in using such a service, it may be worthwhile if a lot of your customers pay by check. You can determine the value of such a service by figuring out how much you lose each year in bad checks and comparing it to the fees charged by the check verification company. If you lose a lot more than it would cost, it may be worthwhile to subscribe to the service. Keep in mind, however, that your fees may go up if the company winds up making good on too many bounced checks.

The other area of concern is if thieves should target your business checking account by producing fraudulent checks with your account number on them. In order to make this kind of scam work, thieves often target large, well-known businesses whose checks are unlikely to be questioned, such as a Kmart or a Safeway. They can then pass off bogus payroll checks drawn on the accounts of those companies. If they try it in a small town, however, the bank tellers are likely to be familiar with such checks. If the checks look odd, they may investigate further before cashing them, thus thwarting the thieves. However, if the thief knows the company's correct account number – because he is a former employee or because the information was passed on by a friend or sold by an acquaintance who is a legitimate employee – it is easier to make the checks appear real. Protect yourself by purchasing your business checks from a reputable check printing company that incorporates the check-fraud prevention features that cannot be duplicated with desktop technology.

Any store, regardless of size, can be targeted by thieves who come across a check issued to a customer as a refund. It is a good idea for the business to maintain a separate checking account on which only refund checks are drawn – all other operating expenses go through the regular business account. The checks drawn on the refund account should have a limit on the funds that can come from that account, and a notice should appear on the check: "Not good for more than $300," or whatever ceiling makes sense for your store. If someone does duplicate the check using desktop technology, the losses will be very small. It is also likely that you can make arrangements with the bank to notify you or to prevent payment of sums of money over a specified dollar amount from the special refund account, which can stop a bad check before your bank pays out on it.

Con Games

In an effort to pass a bad check, professional thieves may try to distract you by approaching the cashier when she is very busy and trying to push her into completing the transaction quickly, without looking carefully at the check. They may also talk quickly or complain about slow service. An overly friendly customer who is unknown to the clerk, yet uses her first name; is overly complimentary; or drops the names of other employees or important people may also be up to no good.

Do not allow exceptions to the policies you have established for accepting checks, especially when the cashier is being intimidated by a pushy customer.

Most of the checks retail operators will see are personal checks, or occasionally, business checks. These are checks drawn on bank accounts that are opened for either an individual or a company. Banks vary in strictness about opening accounts. In big cities, where fraud is common, they often scrutinize and verify the information depositors provide before opening an account. In less crowded areas, banks may be more informal.

Professional thieves know about bank policies and use them to their advantage. One scam they use is to open a checking account (often using a bad check as an opening deposit) for a certain amount of money – say, $500. They then write checks for just under $500 at as many stores as they can get to. Before the bad checks hit their account for payment, they withdraw the $500 – ripping off the bank for good measure – and take their show on the road. By the time the checks written to merchants appear at the bank for payment, the account has been closed, and the initial deposit long gone, leaving the stores with no way to collect on the bad checks. Crooks often work one area for a short period of time before things get too hot and they move on to another jurisdiction for a repeat performance.

Thieves also play con games with altered or counterfeit money orders by presenting them for more than the amount of purchase, such as a $300 money order to pay for a $15 item. They'll ask for the difference back in cash. If you give it to them, you won't be able to collect anything from the issuing bank or the post office, and both your merchandise and cash will be gone for good.

Honest Mistakes

Sometimes you will take all the necessary precautions, but a check will still be returned to you. A number of returned checks are not paid because the account holder has insufficient funds in the bank. Often, there is nothing sinister going on. Most of the time, the person who has written the check has made an mathematical error or has "floated" the check, counting on money expected to be deposited (such as a paycheck) in time to cover the check. People who have checking accounts for most of their adult lives will probably unintentionally bounce a check sooner or later, so an occasional customer error can be understood. Legitimate customers who make mistakes are generally horribly embarrassed and make the uncollected check good right away, often without complaining about paying the store an additional sum to cover the business's bank fees. These people pose no problem to a store owner. It's the scam artists who cause the difficulties.

Customers can also close their accounts before your check is presented. Sometimes this happens because checks drawn on that account were stolen, in which case it should be easy to rectify the bad check. Other times, one member of a couple that is splitting up may clean out the account without the other person's knowledge, in which case it may be harder to recover the money for the bounced check, especially if the check writer does not have other funds available to make it good.

Collection Procedures

When checks are returned to you, they have not reached the end of the road. You have several options, which will vary from state to state, to collect the money owed your store.

The first, of course, is to contact the customer to let him or her know that the bank has returned the check to you unpaid and to make arrangements to collect the money. Insist that the payment be made in cash or with a postal money order. *Do not accept a replacement check.* You also may want to think twice about accepting another check from that customer for future purchases.

In many states, you also have the right to charge the customer a "bounced-check fee" in addition to the face amount of the check. Most banks charge your business account for each check that is returned unpaid, and you may be entitled to pass that fee along to the customer.

If you are unable to contact the customer to make payment arrangements, or if the check-writer has made several promises to bring you the money and has not shown up, you also have the option of redepositing the check. You can deposit a check twice. If it is returned unpaid by the bank the second time, you can bring the check to the bank in person to collect on it. If you decide to do this, it's a good idea to contact the bank on which the check is drawn early each morning to inquire whether there is enough money in the account to cover the check. If so, bring the check in immediately before money can be withdrawn from the account, causing the balance to fall below what is necessary to cover the face amount of the check.

If a check-writer does not make good on a check and you are unable to get the money directly from the bank because, for example, the bank is too far away or the account has been closed, you can either take steps to try to collect the money yourself, or you can turn it over to a collection agency. The rules for collection of a debt are complicated and vary from state to state. It is certainly more convenient to turn the problem over to a collection agency that specializes in this area. The agency will take a percentage of the amount collected as a fee, but recovering most of the money is better than getting beat for the whole amount.

If you want to try collecting on the check yourself, the simplest way of going about it is by using an electronic helper, such as the *Bad Check Recovery Program* on CD-ROM for Windows (ISBN: 1-889031-39-9) from Looseleaf Law Publications (www.LooseleafLaw.com). This software takes the user through three easy steps, which have an 85-percent success rate. If you are unsuccessful in recovering the money, the program allows you to print a statement in order to advance the process into the legal system. The *Bad Check Recovery Program* is tailored to meet the legal requirements of each state because the collection laws vary so widely, and the potential exists for store owners to get into hot water by inadvertently doing something they didn't know was illegal.

Once it becomes clear that a check writer has defrauded you, such as with a non-existent account, turn over the check and any other evidence to police or the prosecutor. It is only by prosecuting thieves who victimize you that you will discourage them and others from targeting your store in the future.

However, whether the local law enforcement authorities spend any time on your case depends on where you live and the severity of the crime. If you are in a large city and you show up with a bad $25 check, chances are slim that the overworked prosecutors or police will be able to devote much time to your case. However, even if you think that the authorities will not take an interest in your bad check, bring it to their attention anyway. It may be a link in a larger scam that police wouldn't find out about without your cooperation.

Chapter 6
CREDIT CARD FRAUD PREVENTION

I
n this electronic age, customers make many of their purchases by credit card, which is convenient both for them and for the store. But these transactions carry an element of risk for retailers, who may wind up absorbing the cost of fraudulent credit card usage. To reduce your chances of being scammed, there are some steps you can take to protect your business.

Authenticating a Credit Card

Advanced technology pairs up with old-fashioned dishonesty when it comes to credit card transactions. It is possible for thieves to create bogus credit cards, which are not attached to any account, for the purpose of "purchasing" goods for which merchants can never recover the money. However, the credit card issuers have developed some anti-fraud designs that will tip off an alert cashier to the fact that a card is not authentic.

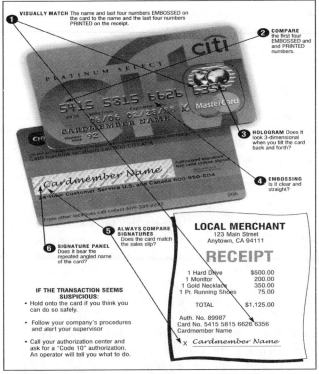

Figure 6.1

The first thing to consider when determining whether a credit card is legitimate is the card number itself. Major credit card numbers are between thirteen and sixteen digits. The last digit is called a "check digit," which is used as part of a complicated mathematical formula to determine whether the rest of the card number is legitimate. The first four digits tell you what kind of card it is: American Express cards start with numbers from 3400 to 3499 or from 3700 to 3799; Discover cards begin with 6011; MasterCards start with numbers from 5100 to 5599; and the first four numbers of Visa cards range from 4000 to 4999. Your bank or credit card processing service can supply more materials and information.

To ensure that what you are looking at is a legitimate credit card, and not something stamped out of plastic in somebody's basement, check the raised numbers and letters. The embossing should be clear and straight. If it's not, that could be a sign that the card is a fake.

In addition, many card issuers print the same first four digits on the card just beneath the first four embossed numbers. The four printed digits should match the embossed numbers.

Many cards also have a hologram. On a real credit card, it appears three-dimensional, not flat.

Look for the small embossed symbol to the right of the expiration date, such as the angled "V" that appears on Visa cards, the "M" on MasterCards, or the "AX" on American Express cards.

Once the sale goes through, compare the customer's name and the last four embossed digits of the card number with the name and the digits that appear on the sales slip printout. It is possible to alter the magnetic stripe or the front of the card so that the information doesn't match – a clear tip-off that the card is no good.

Also, the customer's signature on the sales slip must match the one on the card. The cashier should hold onto the card until after the purchaser has signed the slip in front of him or her. If there is no signature on the strip on the back of the credit card, the clerk should request to see a piece of identification with the person's signature already on it, such as a driver's license, for comparison.

Most merchants today use a POS (point of sale) terminal to process charges. The cashier swipes the card through and keys in the amount of the sale. The machine reads the information about the card from the magnetic stripe. If the stripe isn't functional – which can happen for legitimate reasons as well as dishonest ones – the clerk must key in the card information by hand. The cashier should be sure to look for the card's security features and to check the customer's signature. It's also a good idea to keep a "knuckle-buster" (an old-fashioned manual imprinter) around in order to keep an impression of any card whose stripe won't swipe. (Another tip: The terminal could fail to read the card's stripe if the machine isn't hooked up or is malfunctioning.)

If the customer places an order and gives you a credit card number with the intention of paying cash for the item at a later time, use the knuckle-buster to get an imprint of the card, and keep it on file.

Another characteristic of legitimate credit cards is the Card Verification Value code. Different credit card issuers call it by slightly different names, but it all adds up to the same thing: an additional number that is imprinted (not embossed) on a card to help merchants who are taking phone, mail or Internet orders verify that the customer has a legitimate card in hand at the time of the order. For MasterCard and Visa cards, the CVV is a three-digit number imprinted on the signature panel on the back of the card. American Express cards feature a four-digit number printed just above and to the right of the embossed card number on the front. Instead of featuring a number, all Discover Cards print the name of the same bank on the back: Greenwood Trust Company. If you are taking an order from someone who is not standing in front of you, ask the customer for the code, then send it to the card issuer as part of the authorization request. The issuer will check the code to determine its validity and will send the result back along with the authorization. Keep in mind that once the transaction has been completed, you are not allowed to keep or store that code number.

ATM and Debit Cards

Question: What looks like a credit card and acts like a credit card, but is not a credit card?
Answer: A debit card.

Bet you already knew that! But do you understand what a debit card is and how it differs from a credit card?

Because the debit card – which is also called a check card or an ATM card – looks like a credit card and often even bears the Visa or MasterCard logo, many people assume they are one and the same. The fundamental difference, however, is represented in the name of the card: "credit" vs. "debit."

A credit card is basically an unsecured loan that is extended to the cardholder up to a certain pre-determined amount (the credit limit).

Cardholders use the card to make purchases, then pay for the purchases on a monthly basis when they receive the bill from the credit card company. The credit card company pays the merchants for authorized transactions, generally before the customer even gets the bill.

With a debit card, the customer presents the card; the merchant gets an authorization for the purchase; and the money is transferred to the merchant's account. The difference is that there is no loan involved: the money is deducted, or debited, from the customer's bank account immediately, so the customer is paying with funds that he or she already has in the bank. The debit card is the same card that customers use to withdraw funds from their bank accounts through automatic teller machines (ATMs).

Interestingly, it is estimated that over half the shoppers who use plastic pay with a debit card rather than a credit card, perhaps because a debit card is faster and more convenient than writing a check, yet allows the customer to keep track of personal funds without incurring debt or interest charges on a credit card account.

Debit card transactions are processed through the same payment networks that credit card transactions go through, so the payment system works the same way for the store. For the customer, the difference at the point of sale is the option to sign the sales slip, thus treating the transaction like a credit card transaction, or to use the personal identification number (PIN) – the same number used for ATM access. It is important to ask the customer whether he or she wants to treat the card as a "debit" or a "credit" card for the particular transaction. People who pay with debit cards are split about fifty-fifty regarding their preference to input their PIN numbers or to sign the charge slip. Some people prefer to pay via "credit" when using the debit card and sign the slip because some banks do impose a small fee for each debit transaction (similar to an ATM fee). Whether the card presented is a debit or a credit card, cashiers must make the same efforts to verify both the authenticity of the card and the identity of the customer.

Debit card fraud can occur at the store level because of dishonest cashiers. If a cashier observes the PIN number of a customer who pays with a debit card, the cashier could engage in some sleight of hand to keep the card and then use the PIN number to remove cash from the customer's account at ATMs. POS machines should be set up to protect customer privacy, set on a surface that is angled away from the cashier's line of sight.

Cashiers can also take advantage of the fact that with some POS systems, when a refund is made to a customer's debit card, there is no record of the account number to which the refund is sent. The employee making the refund inputs the store's PIN number in order to authorize the refund. A dishonest employee could refund sums to his or her own debit card account at will. It's best to restrict the store's PIN number to managers and to balance the totals from the POS machine to the cash register every day.

Verifying the Identity of a Card User

When accepting a credit card for a purchase, the cashier must verify that the cardholder is who he or she claims to be. It may take a few hours or a few days before a credit card is reported lost or stolen. In that time, opportunistic thieves can use it to purchase all sorts of merchandise that can be sold later on – and merchants can get stuck with the bills.

Common sense should tell you that the name on the card should match the gender of the person presenting it. Sometimes this can be tricky, as with names that can belong to both males and females, such as Leslie or Lee, but often it is a good indicator – very few men are named Sally, for example.

Ethnicity can also provide a clue to the legitimate cardholder's identity, but it is important to tread carefully. It is possible that a Caucasian woman with long blond hair is named Yu Lin Lee, for example, but it isn't very likely. Some thieves may play on a cashier's reluctance to probe by presenting a card that was issued to a person with an incongruous name and acting insulted if the question about its validity should arise.

The cardholder's signature is another clue, although enterprising con artists can practice imitating the signature on the back of a stolen card.

It may seem that the simplest way to be certain of a card user's identity is to ask for photo ID. However, under Visa, MasterCard, and American Express rules, you cannot refuse to make a credit card sale should a customer decline to show you ID. Also, should a customer be willing to give you personal information such as address and telephone numbers, under no circumstances are you allowed to record that information on the credit slip. If your cashiers violate any of the credit card companies' rules, the companies may deny you the privilege of accepting plastic in the future, which could wind up being extremely costly. So make sure all employees who handle credit card transactions are complying with the requirements to stay within the credit card companies' good graces.

It is a little more complicated to verify a cardholder's identity when an order is placed by phone, by mail, or over the Internet. If your store fulfills orders that are not placed face-to-face, extra effort must go into establishing their legitimacy and that of the cardholder. Some credit card issuers impose a penalty for failing to do so. In other cases the store winds up eating the cost of fraudulent transactions – *even if the transaction is approved by the card issuer*. Remember, getting an authorization means only that the account is in good standing – it doesn't mean that the person placing the order is the real account holder or that the card itself is legitimate.

When a customer is not standing in front of you when placing an order, take his or her home and work telephone numbers as well as addresses – then call back to verify the order. If you call and the person who answers the phone doesn't know what you're talking about, it's a rip-off. On the other hand, even if everything checks out, that is not proof that the transaction is authorized.

In addition to getting telephone numbers, ask the person placing the order to give you the expiration date of the card – then include the date in your authorization request. If the expiration date is invalid or missing, that may be a sign that the person placing the order does not have the actual credit card in hand.

It's also a good idea to ask for additional information, such as the bank name that appears on the front of the card, during the transaction. Again, if the person can't give it to you, he or she doesn't have the card in front of him or her.

You can also confirm the order by sending a note to the customer at his or her billing address, as opposed to sending it to the address where the item will be shipped. If you get a phone call from a confused customer who never placed the order, you know something is amiss.

Merchants who accept credit cards have access to the fraud prevention resources provided by the card issuers. Take advantage of the training as well as the verification tools. The Address Verification Service (AVS), for example, allows you to check the cardholder's billing address against the one on file with the card issuer. If you are making a sale to someone who is not present, simply include an AVS request as part of the authorization process. You will receive a result code that indicates whether the addresses match.

Authorizations and Approvals

Most stores today use an electronic POS, or "swipe," terminal to process credit transactions, but some merchants who don't want to invest in a terminal will call the bank or credit card processing company for card authorization and approval.

The electronic or telephone verification request is made for the dollar amount of the customer's purchase – or, in the case of restaurants, gas stations and similar businesses, for "guesstimated" total purchase amounts, factoring in variables such as the amount of the tip or the fill-up. If your business requests approval for a slightly higher or an estimated amount, be aware that the actual charge amount should be submitted right away. The rules applying to such approval amounts vary slightly, but generally speaking, a hold on an amount that is approved but which has no corresponding charge submitted must be removed from the customer's account within seventy-two hours or less.

You also need to be aware that Visa and MasterCard prohibit setting minimum or "floor" amounts of sale when customers pay with plastic. While American Express doesn't prohibit a minimum charge, under AmEx rules, merchants who accept Visa or MasterCard (which do not allow minimum charge amounts) are not allowed to impose a minimum for users of American Express. You are also not allowed to impose a surcharge on the amount of purchase in order to cover your bank processing fees when the customer pays with a Visa or MasterCard. If you accept Visa, MasterCard and American Express, you may not impose a surcharge on AmEx purchases either. Ten states prohibit merchants from imposing a surcharge on any credit card transactions, so be sure you know the law in your jurisdiction.

When you get the approval, it is an indication that the credit amount is available (or that the funds are available, in the case of a debit card) *at that moment.* If you must delay delivery of the merchandise, such as for a back-ordered or custom-made item, you can charge the customer for the item only when you are ready to deliver it. In the case of a delay, it is best to re-verify the availability of the credit or funds prior to shipping the merchandise.

In addition to the dollar-amount approval, you can also request an address verification. There are different levels of verification responses, ranging from "no match" to "zip code matches, but address does not" to "international card, unable to verify" to "match." It's important to know what information your card processor will be able to provide for which cards. To take it one step further, you can also use an online telephone directory or reverse telephone lookup to determine that the address and telephone number of the customer matches the information provided. However, this method is not 100 percent accurate, as Internet directories are sometimes a little slower to be updated. It's also possible that a legitimate cardholder does not have a phone listed in his or her name. In the case of a married couple, for example, the listing is typically in the name of only one spouse.

If there is something fishy about a transaction, you can do a voice authorization over the phone. Call in the card as a "Code 10," which alerts the operator that you have suspicions about the authenticity of the card or the user without having to say so in front of the customer.

If the authorization is declined, or if you are told that it is a "pick-up card" – a card that the merchant is asked to hold onto and send in to the issuer – then don't accept it. A pick-up card is a red flag indicating that the credit card company wants that card off the street. Under no circumstances should you process a transaction for a "pick-up card."

Sometimes credit card companies offer rewards for returning pick-up cards to them; however, you must weigh your actions against the possibility that the person who presented the card to you might be inclined to do you bodily injury. Play it safe; don't risk your own safety over a piece of plastic.

If it is clear that you shouldn't accept a credit card as payment, simply say, "I'm sorry." Then think twice about accepting a second credit card from that person.

It is possible that even if you follow procedure and verify everything to the best of your ability, you will still have a "chargeback." A chargeback occurs when a customer notifies the credit card issuer that there is a problem with the transaction and requests that the amount of the charge be credited back to his or her account. Chargebacks can occur for a number of reasons, including a customer who never receives the goods ordered; a customer who has returned the merchandise, but did not get a credit for it; or because of fraud. It is to your benefit to work with your customers to the best of your ability to resolve any disputes before they contact their credit card issuer to request a chargeback. A merchant who has an excessive number of chargebacks may lose the privilege of being able to accept credit cards, or may be charged additional fees for doing so. Your bank or credit card processing company can give you more information and provide resources to help you limit the number of chargebacks to your account.

It's important to keep excellent records of credit card transactions in case you have to fight a chargeback, or for other reasons, such as a legal demand. Hold onto all your credit card transaction records because credit card companies can request records going back seven years. Also, you may need to produce the records should a customer be sued for divorce or in the case of other legal action: The wife can request charges made by her husband during the previous few years, to see what he's been ordering and who he's been sending gifts to, for example.

Your records are one of the most important ways in which you can protect your business, so start with the basics, such as making sure you have a good machine tape, rather than one that will cause your transaction record to be illegible. It's best to use carbonless charge forms, but if you do use the ones with carbon paper, make sure that the carbons are destroyed, not just thrown away. "Dumpster divers" make a career out of going through business' garbage to find sensitive financial information that they can use to scam credit card holders and others. Also, be sure that your employees do not get any bright ideas about keeping the carbons to use or sell to other criminals.

Warning Signs of Fraud

Dishonest employees sometimes seek work in a busy retail environment for the sole purpose of gathering other people's credit card numbers, which are then used to make unauthorized purchases. These people often work as part of a ring. Aside from keeping credit card transaction carbons, they can glean account numbers by swiping a customer's card through a small device known as a "skimmer." About the size of a pager, the skimmer reads and records the information from a card's magnetic strip. A cashier simply swipes the card through the legitimate POS terminal, then surreptitiously swipes it through the skimmer before returning it to the customer. The cashier is usually paid a small sum for stealing the credit card numbers and turning them over to another member of the crime ring.

If you spot anyone using an unfamiliar device, or if any employee reports receiving a phone call from a caller who asks for customer information, check into it immediately. All employees should be encouraged to report this kind of activity, and any employee found skimming should be prosecuted. If cardholders get wind that their numbers were stolen from your store, it won't be the individual dishonest employee who gets sued – the business will be hauled into court to answer for the employee's actions. An additional incentive for employees to look out for skimmers is that credit card companies often pay a reward for information that leads to the arrest and conviction of anyone involved in the manufacture or use of counterfeit credit cards.

Dishonest customers can also create headaches for retailers. A recent trend is for customers to ask gift companies, such as florists, to enclose cash with the merchandise delivery order, usually when paying by check or charging the order to a credit card. Merchants who have been doing so have lost their shirts. It's a scam by thieves who use bad checks or stolen credit card numbers to swindle the stores. Common sense should tell you that, as a retailer, your company is not set up to be a bank, so you shouldn't give out cash. More importantly, credit card rules prohibit merchants from doing so.

There are other signs that someone may be trying to rip off the store by paying with a *stolen credit card*.

Employees should keep an eye out for customers who

◆ choose items quickly and randomly, without regard to size, color, style or price.

◆ make a purchase, then return later to make another.

◆ question a cashier or floor personnel about the floor price limit .

◆ make several purchases that come close to, but never go over, the floor limit.

◆ insist on taking a large, awkward, or bulky item immediately, rather than waiting to have it delivered.

◆ refuse free clothing alterations.

◆ produce the credit card from a pocket, rather than a wallet or purse.

◆ have a credit card that isn't signed on the back.

◆ are unable to produce ID.

◆ are incongruous in appearance: a down-and-out looking person, for example, ordering things that can be taken with him or her.

◆ rush or distract the cashier, especially during busy times or at closing.

◆ are unnecessarily talkative or friendly, dropping the names of important people or company higher-ups.

◆ act suspicious, especially teenagers who attempt to use a credit card.

Spot *phone* or *Internet* orders that may not be the real McCoy, especially when a new customer places the order.

Beware of the following fishy situations –

◆ Extremely large orders.

◆ A number of deliveries, especially for multiples of the same item, going to the same address.

◆ Orders shipped to a single address but charged to several different credit cards.

◆ Multiple transactions on the same credit card for items to be shipped to different addresses.

◆ Multiple transactions on the same credit card in a short period of time.

◆ Orders to be shipped on a rush basis or via overnight delivery.

◆ Orders going to an international address.

◆ Incongruous names: a customer who claims to be, for example, Bill Smith, yet signs a gift card "Love, Dave."

◆ Incongruous addresses: a person who sounds illiterate, for example, requesting a delivery to a wealthy part of town, or vice-versa.

Chapter 7
CURRENCY: COUNTERFEIT MONEY
AND CASH SCAMS

I n 2001, a record $47.5 million in counterfeit U.S. money entered into circulation, and in 2002, $43 million in fake bills were created and passed. Because of the advances in technology, 39 percent of the bad bills were computer generated – a huge rise over the 0.5 percent that were made by computer in 1995.

In an effort to keep one step ahead of the counterfeiters, as of 2003, the government redesigned U.S. currency once again. The rollout of the new money was set up in a staggered fashion, beginning with the release of the $20 bill in late 2003, and followed by the $50 note in 2004 and the $100 bill in 2005. The $5 and $10 notes may be redesigned at some point in the future, but the $1 and $2 bills will remain the same. As part of the effort to continuously improve currency design and protect the economy, the Federal Reserve System and the Department of the Treasury expect to introduce new currency designs every seven to ten years. You can access the latest information and updates about new currency at www.retailsecurity.biz.

The redesigned notes were created to be safer, smarter and more secure than existing bills. The new look includes enhanced security features and other new designs, including a subtle introduction of color, which will make it more burdensome to counterfeit and easier to distinguish denominations. The old money will continue to be used, and the new bills will co-circulate with older series notes. As the new currency is phased in, the old notes will be retired by the Federal Reserve when they are returned through the banking system.

Getting used to the look of new money is a challenge that everyone who uses U.S. currency will have to meet. To avoid being the victim of enterprising criminals, it's important that your staff is knowledgeable about the features and designs of both the older as well as the new bills. In addition, cashiers have to keep an eye out for con artists who are still pulling oldie-but-goodie cash scams and trying out new ones every day.

Identifying the New Bills

The government has drawn on technology in redesigning the currency. Surprisingly, however, the Secret Service says that the best way to determine whether you're holding a real bill or a counterfeit is not to rely on technological devices, such as counterfeit detector pens, but to lean on your own personal counterfeit detectors: your eyes and fingers.

Get to know the characteristics of each bill, especially $20s, $50s and $100s, which are the most widely circulated, both by counterfeiters and legitimate customers. Take a bill that you know is genuine, and compare other bills to it. Do they both look and feel the same? That's the key to knowing whether someone is trying to pass off a bogus bill. Currency that is computer-generated also has black, pink, blue and yellow dots scattered throughout both sides of the bills.

The most notable difference between older series notes and the newly redesigned bills is the use of color. The introduction of colors other than green or black is historic – it is the first time in modern U.S. history that the currency deviates from the traditional "greenback" look. Different background colors will be used on different denominations.

$20 Bill – 2003

In addition to color, several other security features have been incorporated into the new $20 (See Figure 7.1). Make sure that everyone on your staff has an opportunity to study a genuine, redesigned $20 bill and becomes familiar with these new security and design features:

♦ **Color.** Subtle green, peach and blue hues are featured in the background on both sides. The words "TWENTY USA" have been printed in blue in the background to the right of the portrait. Small yellow numeral 20s have been printed in the background on the back of the bill.

♦ **Symbols of freedom.** Two new American eagle "symbols of freedom" appear on the front of the note. The large blue eagle in the background to the left of President Andrew Jackson's portrait is representative of those drawn and sculpted during his time period. The smaller metallic eagle to the lower right of the portrait is a more contemporary illustration, using the same "raised ink" intaglio process as the portrait, numerals and engraving. (The symbols of freedom differ for each denomination.)

♦ **Updated portrait and vignette.** Oval borders and fine lines surrounding the portrait on the front and the White House vignette on the back of the note have been removed. The portrait has been moved up and shoulders have been extended into the border. Additional engraving details have been added to the vignette background.

THE NEW COLOR OF MONEY
Safer, Smarter, More Secure

THE NEW $20 DESIGN retains three important security features that were first introduced in the 1990s and are easy for consumers and merchants alike to check: **WATERMARK, COLOR-SHIFTING INK**, and **SECURITY THREAD**.

SECURITY THREAD

Hold the bill up to the light and look for the security thread, or plastic strip, that is embedded in the paper and runs vertically up one side of the note. If you look closely, the words "USA TWENTY" and a small flag are visible along the thread from both sides of the note.

COLOR-SHIFTING INK

Look at the number "20" in the lower right corner on the face of the bill. When you tilt the note up and down, the color-shifting ink changes color from copper to green.

WATERMARK

Hold the bill up to the light and look for the watermark, or faint image, similar to the large portrait. The watermark is part of the paper itself and can be seen from both sides of the note.

Figure 7.1

◆ **Watermark.** A watermark, or faint image, similar to the large portrait can be seen from both sides of the note. The best way to spot it is to hold the bill up to the light. The watermark is a part of the paper itself.

◆ **Security thread.** A plastic strip, or security thread, is embedded in the paper and runs vertically up one side of the note. The words "USA TWENTY" and a small flag are visible along the thread from both sides of the note. The security thread is most easily spotted when the bill is held up to the light. The security thread will also glow green when placed under ultraviolet light.

◆ **Color-shifting ink.** The number "20" in the lower right corner on the face of the bill is printed in color-shifting ink. When the note is tilted up and down, the ink changes from copper to green. This color shift is more dramatic in the new $20, which makes it even easier to determine the legitimacy of a bill.

◆ **Microprinting.** Microprinted words are so tiny that they are very hard to replicate. The redesigned currency features microprinting on the face of the note in two new areas. Bordering the first three letters of the "TWENTY USA" ribbon to the right of the portrait, the inscription "USA 20" is microprinted in blue. The words "THE UNITED STATES OF AMERICA 20 USA 20" are microprinted in black on the border below the Treasurer's signature.

◆ **Low-vision feature.** The large numeral "20" in the lower right corner on the back of the bill is easy to read.

◆ **Federal Reserve Indicators.** A universal seal to the left of the portrait represents the entire Federal Reserve System. A letter and number beneath the left serial number identifies the issuing Federal Reserve Bank.

◆ **Serial numbers.** The unique combination of eleven numbers and letters appears twice on the front of the note.

Currency Prior to 2003

The redesigned U.S. currency that was printed until 2003 incorporated several security features designed both to help people differentiate the denominations and to combat counterfeiting. Because these bills will be in circulation for a long time, it is important for everyone who handles cash to be familiar with their unique characteristics (See Figure 7.2):

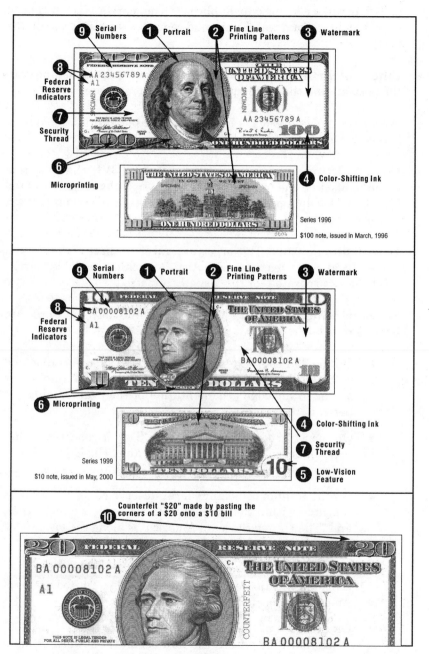

Figure 7.2

◆ **Portrait.** The enlarged portraits are easier to recognize, while the added detail is harder to duplicate. The portrait is off-center, providing room for a watermark and reducing wear and tear on the portrait.

◆ **Fine Line Printing Patterns.** The fine lines printed behind both the portrait and the building are difficult to replicate.

◆ **Watermark.** A watermark identical to the portrait is visible from both sides when held up to a light.

◆ **Color-Shifting Ink.** Optically variable ink (OVI) changes from green to black in the number in the lower right-hand corner of the bill when viewed from different angles. There is no color-shifting ink on the $5 note.

◆ **Low-Vision Feature.** The large numeral on the back of the $5, $10, $20 and $50 note is easy to read. Also, a machine-readable feature has been incorporated for the visually impaired.

◆ **Microprinting.** Because they're so small, microprinted words are hard to replicate.

  ◆ On the $5 Federal Reserve Note, "Five Dollars" is repeated on both side borders, and "The United States of America" is on the lower edge ornamentation of the oval framing the portrait.

  ◆ On the $10 Federal Reserve Note, "Ten" is repeated within the number in the lower left corner and "The United States of America" is repeated just above Hamilton's name.

  ◆ On the front of the $20 Federal Reserve Note, "USA 20" is repeated within the number in the lower left-hand corner, and "The United States of America" is along the lower edge ornamentation of the oval framing the portrait.

  ◆ On the $50 Federal Reserve Note, the word "Fifty" is repeated within the side borders, and "The United States of America" is located on Grant's collar.

  ◆ On the front of the $100 Federal Reserve Note, "USA 100" is microprinted within the number in the lower left-hand corner, while "The United States of America" appears on Benjamin Franklin's lapel.

- **Security Thread.** A clear, inscribed polyester thread is incorporated into the paper of genuine currency.

  - The thread is embedded in the paper and runs vertically through the clear field to the left of the portrait on the $5 denomination. This thread glows blue when held under an ultraviolet light. On the $5 Federal Reserve Note, the words "USA FIVE" and a flag can be seen from both sides of the light. The number "5" appears in the star field of the flag.

  - A vertically embedded thread to the right of the portrait indicates the $10 denomination. The words "USA TEN" and a flag can be seen from both sides against a light. The number "10" appears in the star field of the flag. The thread glows orange under an ultraviolet light.

  - The thread is embedded in the paper and runs vertically through the clear field to the left of the portrait on the $20 denomination. This thread glows green when held under an ultraviolet light. On the $20 Federal Reserve Note, the words "USA TWENTY" are repeated along the entire length of the security thread.

  - The $50 Federal Reserve Note has its security thread embedded vertically in the paper to the right of the portrait. The words "USA 50" and a flag can be seen from both sides of the note when held up to a bright light. This thread glows yellow when held under an ultraviolet light.

  - The $100 Federal Reserve Note has its security thread embedded vertically in the paper to the left of the portrait. The words "USA 100" can be seen from both sides of the note when held up to a bright light. This thread glows light red/pink when held under an ultraviolet light.

- **Federal Reserve Indicators.** A new universal seal represents the entire Federal Reserve System. A letter and number beneath the left serial number identify the issuing Federal Reserve Bank, along with the second letter of the serial number.

- **Serial Numbers.** An additional letter has been added to the front of the serial number. The unique combination of eleven numbers and letters appears twice on the front of the note. 1996 series begin with the letter A. 1999 series begin with the letter B.

(Information provided by the United States Secret Service.)

Myths and Truths About Recognition Methods

It's tempting to hand every cashier a detector pen and instruct them to mark each bill as they receive it, but, despite what the pen manufacturers would have you believe, that doesn't really help you distinguish good bills from bad.

Common sense should tell you that a pen can't take into account all the characteristics of a note and determine whether it's legitimate or not. The way the pens work is that they contain a chemical – usually an iodine solution – that will react with the starch in wood-based paper (such as photocopier or laser printer paper) to create a stain. If the pen is applied to the fiber-based paper used in real bills, no discoloration is supposed to occur. However, false positives and false negatives are common. If there is starch present on a real bill, for example, it will fail the counterfeit detection pen test – but that doesn't mean it's a fake. Likewise, you can apply the pen to a sheet of linen stationery, and it's likely that no discoloration will appear, but that doesn't make the writing paper genuine currency.

To avoid being duped, everyone who handles cash, including cashiers and employees who make bank deposits or change the store's money at a bank, should study each denomination until they are familiar with their characteristics, then look carefully at and use their fingers to feel each bill that customers or tellers hand them. Criminals often wait for peak times, when cashiers are busiest, to try to pass off bogus bills. Everyone wants the lines to move quickly, but it is worth the extra seconds it will take employees to evaluate each bill to be sure that it's the real thing. Thieves have been known to cut the corners of higher-denomination bills off and glue them onto bills of lower value (corners from $20 bills, for example, pasted onto a $1 or even a $10 bill). (See figure 7.2) At first glance, the numeral "20" in the corners will jump out at the receiver, but that extra moment's examination will reveal George Washington's portrait in the middle, rather than Andrew Jackson's, and the denomination written out at the bottom of the note on both the front and the back, as well as through the treasury seal. "Raised" bills are also considered counterfeit.

Two devices that are helpful in determining the legitimacy of cash, as well as checks, travelers checks, and credit cards, are a 10x-power magnifying glass and an ultraviolet light. Both of these items are inexpensive enough to provide one of each at every cash register. They come in hand-held as well as desktop models, both of which are small and portable.

If, after examining a bill, there is still question about its legitimacy – whether it's from a customer, a bank teller, or anyone else – you have the right to refuse it. Simply say, "I don't like this bill. Could you give me another one, please?"

What to Do If You Receive Counterfeit Money

If you do get stuck with a counterfeit bill, you've just become engaged in a game of hot potato in which you're the loser. Whoever discovers that the buck is bogus has to eat the amount because the government won't take a loss on counterfeit currency. And before you get any clever ideas about trying to stick the next guy with the fake note, keep in mind that if you try to pass counterfeit money in order to avoid taking a loss, you are participating in a felony. Clearly, being slapped with a hefty fine or serving up to ten years in prison are not worthwhile tradeoffs, regardless of the denomination of the bad bill you've taken in.

Even if you receive the counterfeit from a bank that has unwittingly given it to you, the bank is not obligated to replace it with a genuine one. The flip side is that if your store dispenses a bogus note because of a genuine error, you don't have to make good on it, either. Of course, in the interest of good customer relations, you can let the customer know that you are going above and beyond by compensating him or her, anyway.

If you do find yourself the recipient of a counterfeit bill, you'll have to turn it over to the authorities. Don't return it to the passer. Handle the suspect note as little as possible, but do write your initials and the date in the white border areas. Carefully place it in a protective covering, such as an envelope, and obtain the number for your local police department or the local field office for the U.S. Secret Service from the information operator or the front page of your local telephone directory. The Secret Service has field offices in every state, plus Washington, D.C., and Puerto Rico, as well as overseas, including several in Canada, and in various Latin American, European and Asian countries.

The authorities will send someone to pick up the bill. Be sure that you examine the person's identification carefully before handing over the note. If you have any doubts about the person's affiliation with a law enforcement agency, look up the telephone number of the agency yourself (don't call a number he or she gives you), and ask them to verify that the person works for them and was sent to your store by them to pick up the bill.

If you can give the authorities a description of the person who passed the note, it will be helpful. If at all possible to do so without endangering anyone, try to delay the passer until a law enforcement officer arrives. If not, memorize the passer's description, as well as that of any companions, and try to get the description and license numbers of any vehicles they use.

Don't fall victim to the counterfeit scam wherein someone appears at your store and represents himself as a police officer or member of the Secret Service. In this swindle, the con artist says he has information that you have received some counterfeit money and that he is here to take custody of it. He offers to give a receipt for the money you turn over. Obviously, the "receipt" is worthless, and you will never see your money again. If this should happen, demand that the person produce his credentials, then call the agency that he purports to work for (again, *you* look up the number – don't call the number that the person gives you, or you'll wind up "confirming" his identity with his accomplice) and let them know what's going on. Real law enforcement agencies don't send representatives to businesses to take their cash.

Legal Reproduction of U.S. Currency

It is interesting to note that not all reproductions of U.S. currency are illegal. In fact, it's okay to reproduce money in commercial advertisements, provided they conform to size and color restrictions. According to the U.S. Secret Service, "photographic and other likenesses of U.S. obligations and securities and foreign currencies are permissible for any non-fraudulent purpose, provided that the items are

◆ reproduced in black and white, and

◆ are less than three-quarters (75 percent) or greater than one-and-one-half times the size, in linear dimension, of any part of the original item being reproduced.

"Negatives and plates used in making the likenesses must be destroyed after their use for the purpose for which they were made.

"Motion picture films, microfilms, videotapes, and slides of paper currency, securities, and other obligations may be made in color or black and white for projection or telecasting. No prints may be made from these unless they conform to the size and color restrictions.

"Photographs, printed illustrations, motion picture film, or slides of United States and foreign coins may be used for any purpose.

"With few exceptions, existing law generally prohibits the manufacture, sale, or use of any token, disk, or device in the likeness or similitude of any coins of the United States, or of any foreign country, which are issued as money."

Till Tapping

Till tapping, or till dipping, is a crude form of cash theft that involves the outright stealing of money from the register while the cashier's attention is diverted elsewhere. The con artists who practice till dipping will drop something on the cashier's side of the counter, spill something, or otherwise try to distract the cashier from an open cash drawer. While the cashier's focus is away from the register, the thief reaches in and grabs a fistful of bills. If two crooks are in on it, one will distract the cashier while the other snatches the cash.

Change Cons

Con artists depend on fast talking and confusion to pull their tricks and leave before the victim catches on. One way they can rip off a store is by causing chaos at the register.

The key to the short-change con is to get the cashier to allow the thief to hold both the thief's money and the store's at the same time, and dupe the cashier into thinking that nothing is amiss. A con artist running this game will wait until the register drawer is open, then ask for change – say, a bunch of twenties in exchange for two $100 bills. If the cashier gives the thief the hundreds, then counts the twenties, she will realize that there is one missing. The trickster will claim the cashier is mistaken and ask to count the bills for himself. Upon "discovering" that there is a bill missing, he will produce the missing note, then request four $50 bills instead, and give the cashier the twenties. The only problem is that the thief leaves with both the hundreds and the fifties. In the confusion, the cashier may not even realize what has happened until the drawer is balanced at the end of the day.

To avoid becoming a victim of the short-change scam, cashiers should be instructed to count the money that the customer hands over *before* giving out other bills in exchange. In addition, the cashier must close the register drawer after every transaction. If the customer requests an additional cash exchange, it should be treated as a separate transaction. The cashier should also make sure that they never allow a customer to hold both the store's and the customer's own money at the same time.

If a customer claims that a cashier has short-changed him, close the register and balance the drawer immediately. If it isn't possible to do so, take the customer's name and contact information and promise to get in touch with him at the end of the shift, when the drawer is balanced. Should the customer be correct, you can return the money at that time. If the person is trying to rip off the store, you can be sure that the name and information he provides will be bogus.

Another scam that can occur happens when thieves work together in pairs. One gets on line just ahead of the other and pays for a purchase with a high-value bill that is marked in some distinctive way. When the second con artist gets to the register, he pays with a bill of a smaller denomination. When he receives the change, he claims that, in fact, he had paid with the larger bill (which his friend had actually given to the cashier just before), and that the amount of change is incorrect. He claims that he remembers giving the cashier the higher-value note because it had a name, date, saying, or other distinctive marking penned on it, and asks the cashier to open the drawer to check. Sure enough, the marked bill will be right where the trickster said it would be.

To avoid having to give the thief the benefit of the doubt – and the money – cashiers should place the money received on the ledge of the register until the customer has counted the change and the transaction has been completed. If the employee has already made the error, close out the drawer and count it out immediately, or take the customer's name and contact information to use when the shift is over and the register balanced.

Chapter 8
REFUND AND EXCHANGE SCAMS AND ERRORS

T here is plenty of opportunity for loss when issuing refunds or allowing customers to exchange merchandise. Some of it can occur because of human error – either on the part of the customer or on the part of the employee – but some of it is due to customer dishonesty.

One feature of good service is to allow exchanges and refunds to take place easily, without inconveniencing the customer. Thieves sometimes take advantage of hassle-free return policies to steal from the store. A good way to strike a balance between keeping legitimate customers happy and crooks away is to establish a policy, post it near the registers – then stick to it. If there's enough room on the receipt to print the policy there as well, so much the better.

Of course, consumer laws vary from state to state, and you may be obligated to provide refunds or exchanges for particular reasons or within specified periods of time under state and federal statutes. Be sure that you are familiar with these requirements and that you incorporate them into your store policies.

As long as you post the store's refund and exchange policy at the register, you take the wind out of the sails of any customers who claim that they didn't know the rules, and it allows you to eliminate many cases of attempted customer fraud.

Cash Refunds

Some enterprising thieves scour the floors inside the store, the parking lot, or the trash bins outside the store for discarded receipts. They pull the items corresponding to those listed on the receipt off the shelves and attempt to "return" them for an on-the-spot cash refund. More resourceful crooks obtain receipts that have been thrown away or actually make a legitimate purchase in order to get one, then photocopy or scan and print many copies of the receipt. They use these copies to keep "returning" stolen merchandise for cash refunds. One way to discourage the copied or "found" receipts scam is to use different color register tapes on different days, or to use sequentially numbered sales tickets kept on file or whose numbers are recorded.

Cashiers or other employees who process refunds must be trained to verify the amount of the refund against the price of the item when it was sold. If a customer requests a refund for an item that retails at full price for $50, but which she purchased at the sale price of $30, the cashier has to be certain that the item was not sold for the sale price, or the store will be out $20. If your POS system utilizes scanning devices, and the item is no longer on sale or the price has gone up since the customer bought the merchandise, the higher price will display. It's important for the cashier to examine the original receipt to ensure that the correct amount is refunded. When selling a marked-down item, cashiers should be required to cross out the full price and write in the sale price so that it's obvious how much the customer has paid for the product.

If your store issues coupons that entitle the customer to a certain amount off if the total price of all items is over a certain amount – say, $25 off an order of $100 or more – make sure that you have a way to recall the original transaction in case the person returns one item and requests a refund. As an example, someone buys two items – one for $100 and one for $30 – for a total of $130, and receives the $25 off for presenting the coupon, thus paying a total of $105. The customer then returns the item that costs $100 and requests a refund for it. Without examining the original receipt carefully or reviewing the original transaction, the cashier will refund the $100 in its entirety, thus depriving the store of $25. After receiving the refund, the customer has, in effect, paid only $5 for the $30 product because the value of the $25-off coupon was not factored into the refund.

Whether your store policy dictates that the customer must present a receipt in order to get a refund or can obtain cash back without a sales slip, it's best to issue the refund by mail if the purchase was paid for by check. The store could be burned by issuing cash refunds if someone pays with a rubber check – whether they bounce it intentionally or in error – but returns the merchandise before the check clears the bank. If you give back the purchase price in cash, the store loses both the cash and the original amount written on the bad check.

It's also smart to establish a cash refund ceiling: for refunds over a certain amount, the store will not issue refunds in cash, but will send a refund by mail. It's best not to post the ceiling amount, however, so that thieves do not grab items whose prices are just under the limit in order to qualify for the cash refund.

Returning and Exchanging Stolen Merchandise

Crafty shoplifters have also been known to steal an item from one store and attempt to return it to another store in the same chain for a cash refund. The bolder ones simply lift an item and bring it over to the counter for a refund without even leaving the store with it first. If you require identification giving the person's name and address in order to mail a refund check to them, many thieves, who want to avoid being identified, will leave the store, acting like an unhappy customer – but without the cash refund.

Shoplifters may also bring in a stolen product without a receipt and ask to exchange it for an identical item in a different size or color. They come by the merchandise either by shoplifting it from another store in the same chain, or from friends who sell large quantities of merchandise that "fell off the back of a truck" to them at reduced prices. They will want to get the store to issue them a receipt for this new item so that they can turn around and bring it into another store for a cash refund. If you do give a customer a receipt for an exchanged item, be sure to write on it that the receipt was not issued for the original purchase.

Another exchange scam that thieves engage in is a variation of distraction theft which occurs during a return or exchange. Usually, the bad guys work in pairs to pull this con. They bring in an item, ostensibly to return it or exchange it for another piece of merchandise. One member of the pair engages the employee's attention or distracts the employee. Meanwhile, the other thief replaces the genuine item that was brought in for return or exchange with a counterfeit one. When the employee turns his or her attention back to the item, he or she doesn't realize that it is not the original one that was presented. Employees who work with small, expensive items, such as jewelry, are often most vulnerable to this scam. To avoid being taken, they should be instructed never to leave merchandise unattended for any reason.

Credit Vouchers

Credit vouchers are a good compromise when a customer wants to return an item without a sales slip; when the return is attempted a fairly long time after the original purchase was made; when customers can't produce receipts because the merchandise was given to them as gifts; or when the items were bought by a third party, who paid for them with a check or credit card. The voucher allows the person to return the item they don't want and select something else, yet the store does not have to part with any money to keep the customer happy.

Dishonest people generally do not want to have to fill out forms or show identification when pulling a scam, so issuing a credit voucher will help eliminate fraud. As with refund forms, credit vouchers should be numbered sequentially and require the signature of a manager or supervisor to be issued. Keep track of the recipients, and take a look at any repeat customers. Also pay attention to the clerks who initiate these credits. If one employee is particularly active in this area, it could be a sign that the person is issuing fraudulent vouchers and using them or passing them on to friends who redeem them for merchandise.

The Importance of Keeping a Log

As with other cash management functions, a manager or supervisor should be required to authorize and countersign any refunds. Customer signatures should also be required on the refund slip. It's best to use sequentially numbered refund vouchers and to log in any refunds issued on a daily basis. Keep copies of the refund slips in a log or a file, and review them at regular intervals.

It's also a good idea to establish a database of refund recipients. This can be done simply and easily by using a desktop computer. By cross-checking the names and addresses, you can spot any repeat "customers." If someone's name appears more than once, a manager should review all the refund transactions. If the same item is being refunded several times – especially if the person hasn't presented a sales slip for it – it's a sign that the person may be committing fraud. To put an end to it, you can call and let the person know that they have appeared on the store's radar screen. Inquire what the problem might be with the product, and let the individual know that this is the last refund that the store will issue without a sales receipt. You can also ask for the date that the item was purchased and check the store records for that day to see whether that item was really sold on that date. If the person is stealing from the store, a phone call is usually enough to let him or her know that the game is over.

If the same address appears on several refunds, that also bears investigation. Go through the personnel records, or use an Internet-based reverse directory to determine whether an employee might be supplementing his or her income by mailing store refund checks home.

If a particular employee or several employees seem to be responsible for initiating most of the refunds, take a harder look to determine whether all of the refunds are legitimate. Also, double-check any vouchers that are processed out of sequence. This could be an indication that employees are falsifying a manager's signature.

A good supervisory technique that does double-duty as refund verification and customer service is to follow up with mail and/or phone calls inquiring about the customer's experience. Send out a letter or post card to all customers who receive refunds, asking questions such as, "Was your refund handled promptly? Did our employees extend courteous service to you during the refund transaction? Would you shop in our store again?" As an incentive for the customer to respond, the store can offer a $5 coupon good toward the customer's next purchase. Mail that is returned because the address doesn't exist, or because no one with that name lives at the address, indicates that something is fishy. Further investigation is warranted.

Likewise, managers or supervisors should pull refund vouchers out at random intervals and call the recipients, especially those who have received a high-dollar amount back. If someone professes not to know anything about receiving any refunds, there is a problem. If the refunds are legitimate, it offers managers an opportunity to impress upon the customers how important their business is to the store.

Chapter 9
VENDOR FRAUD AND RECEIVING VULNERABILITIES

A lot of loss that occurs actually exists only on paper. Clerical errors, especially regarding merchandise receiving, are easy to make if the proper procedures aren't set up and followed by employees. In addition, the loading dock and receiving areas, by their very nature, are places where the store is vulnerable to actual merchandise theft. Unscrupulous vendors and delivery personnel are also responsible for a certain amount of loss.

Fortunately, good clerical and oversight procedures can help eliminate a great deal of the loss resulting from dishonest suppliers and unprotected receiving areas. The key is setting up the proper procedures and ensuring employee compliance.

Loading Dock and Receiving Area Vulnerability

The loading dock and receiving areas are juicy targets for thieves because that's where merchandise can be found in bulk. Whether they're looking to make off with whole pallets of products, or just want to sneak a few items out at a time, crooks are attracted to where the goods are. A thief who steals from loading or receiving areas could be an outside individual just looking for a score, but it is more often an employee or someone who has regular access to the area, such as a truck driver who delivers for an established supplier. Someone who is familiar with the layout and the routine is in a better position to steal than someone who walks in cold, hoping to get lucky.

As with other types of thefts, reducing or removing the opportunity is an important part of loss control in shipping and receiving. Loading and receiving areas should be separate places. If there is only one area for goods to be moved in and out, accidental or intentional losses could occur in the confusion.

An important step is to control human traffic in these areas by establishing regular receiving days and hours. A supplier who fails to deliver during those times should be notified that your store will refuse to accept responsibility for any shipment left without being checked in according to procedure. Require that deliveries be made only via the designated receiving area – and never through the front door of the store.

The store employee who is in charge of receiving the goods should be the one to check in all merchandise – never allow a driver to "verify" that the entire shipment has been delivered. Also, drivers who complete a delivery are often left alone after the receiver finishes checking it in and goes inside. This is an opportunity for the unscrupulous driver to steal merchandise that has already been delivered and is just sitting there.

The driver or other delivery personnel should be prohibited from removing any empty cartons, whether they have been flattened or not. And under no circumstances should non-store personnel (such as drivers) be allowed to stock store shelves.

Unscrupulous employees can use the chaos of the loading and receiving areas to divert a driver's attention long enough to sneak some cartons away from his shipment. If employees are allowed to hang out in these areas, there is a greater opportunity that they can carry off unauthorized boxes to someone's waiting car or truck – or sneaked into a dumpster for retrieval after hours. Aside from the opportunity for theft, these areas are dangerous, and employees should not be allowed to congregate there.

Access to the shipping and receiving areas should be limited to authorized employees who are working at that moment (not on a break or on a day off), and to authorized vehicles (not an employee's own car, for example). One employee should be responsible for each transaction or shipment and should be required to sign the delivery receipt or transfer ticket to acknowledge that the proper number of items – as well as the right type of goods, and not a cheaper version than the store is being billed for – are accounted for. The driver picking up a shipment should also sign the ticket to verify the count. Only one employee should be responsible for physically transferring the goods, while a manager supervises the transaction. Rotate employees into and out of these assignments on a random, unscheduled basis.

Once the shipment is inside the building or warehouse area and is being reconciled with the manifest or invoice, if it becomes apparent that a shortage, overage or receipt of damaged stock has occurred, it should be reported immediately. The employee responsible for the accounting paperwork should reconcile all shipping and receiving documents and make management aware of any discrepancies.

Storeroom Access

Wherever merchandise is stored, whether in a stockroom or a warehouse, the same principles that hold true for displaying products on the floor should be practiced. Boxes or individual items should be stacked neatly so that any holes will be immediately obvious.

Access to the area should be limited to necessary personnel who are supervised by managers. The best way to restrict access to any area is to limit the number of keys that are floating around and to distribute the keys judiciously. When a key-holder leaves the company, whether on good terms or not, the locks should be re-keyed and new keys made.

Alarms and surveillance equipment are necessary to protect high-dollar items within storerooms as well as on the sales floor.

Attention to Invoice Detail

Paperwork is of utmost importance in keeping accurate shipments and delivery counts. Everyone who handles the papers, from the receiver to the accounting personnel, must pay attention to all the details. While this seems tedious, it is less trouble to spot errors or discrepancies sooner rather than trying to figure out where merchandise got to months later, when the paper trail is cold.

Thieving drivers can take advantage of even the best organized receiver by altering paperwork after the delivery has been checked in and signed for. By changing the number of cartons from "10" to "16" on the packing slip after the receiver has signed for 10, for example, the driver causes the store to be invoiced for 16 and to pay for an extra six boxes of product that were never delivered. The driver can then take those six boxes and sell them on the side, keeping the money for himself.

This kind of shortage can be picked up by an eagle-eyed accounting person during reconciliation. To provide additional safeguards, the use of a logbook is an excellent idea. Every delivery should be recorded in the book, and the paperwork reconciled on a regular basis. This kind of record keeping also helps eliminate the danger that the store will pay twice for a double-billed shipment.

Getting Shorted

A corrupt vendor can short-ship a store at the factory or distribution point, and this does happen, both intentionally and accidentally. However, short shipments are more often attributable to dishonest delivery personnel, who work either alone or in collusion with store receiving employees.

Dishonest drivers can easily deliver a light load to the store if employees are not religious about verifying delivery tickets. If chaos reigns in the receiving area, an unscrupulous driver can also reload some boxes back onto the truck after they've been counted by the store employee. In either case, the driver sells the "extra" merchandise and keeps the profit. Sometimes drivers work within a network of criminals who are set up to fence a large amount of stolen goods. But sometimes they are solo entrepreneurs, who offer the next store on their route a "good deal" on the goods. If a driver offers you a special price on any merchandise, especially if the boxes are in the cab of the truck, rather than in the freight area, it's a good idea to let the vendor or the trucking company know about it. More often than not, they'll appreciate the information.

Supervisors should spot-check shipments just after they've been checked in. If a shortage is apparent, yet the receiver hasn't reported it and has signed the slip indicating that all merchandise was accounted for, the receiver may be working in cahoots with the delivery driver, pulling a shorting scam.

Chapter 10
INSURANCE PROTECTION

I t is vital to have the proper kind and amounts of business insurance coverage. Because insurance isn't a sexy topic, many store owners fall into one of two categories: "I'll think about getting insurance another day," or, "I bought the insurance policy recommended by my agent. I don't know what the provisions are, but I'm sure the store is covered for anything that happens."

Unfortunately, neither of these attitudes toward insurance coverage will help you should the store be involved in a lawsuit, crime, injury or disaster.

Determining Sufficient Coverage

The most basic questions that every retailer needs to ask regarding insurance coverage are

- What kind of coverage do I need?
- How much insurance is the right amount?
- Which additional policies or riders are necessary for my kind of business?
- What deductible amounts make sense for my store?

The kind of insurance you need depends on what kind of store you have and what kind of activities your employees are involved in. Federal and state laws may also require that your type of business carry certain minimums of specific types of insurance.

At a minimum, you should consider liability, workman's compensation, and property insurance. Crime and fraud, vehicle, and employee health coverages are also areas that you should investigate.

Surprisingly, many businesspeople are either unaware of or don't think that business interruption insurance is important. This kind of coverage is what will keep your business going should there be a fire or other disaster that causes you to close for a period of time, so be sure to investigate your options in this area.

It can be demonstrated that sufficient coverage is imperative by considering what an uninsured loss will cost your business. Assuming a sales profit of 5 percent, an uninsured loss of $5,000 will not be made up until the store sells an additional $100,000 of merchandise. Looking at it from this angle, the insurance premiums seem pretty puny when stacked against the potential losses the company could suffer.

Before you sign on the dotted line and hand an agent a premium check, you need to do some basic investigation. The best place to ask questions about recommended business insurance types and levels is your professional association. Many retail organizations have literature or a knowledgeable person on staff who can make recommendations about business insurance policies. The associations draw on information gleaned from the members over a number of years. Associations also often do studies and surveys of their members to find out what they believe is the necessary level of protection. If you ask the organization for assistance, you can draw on a collective database to help you make your decision.

Another good place to go for answers is the horse's mouth: Ask your local competitors and colleagues about what kind of coverage they have, which companies they buy from, and why. Insurance coverage is hardly a trade secret that you could steal from them, so there's no reason why they shouldn't answer your questions. After all, you may be in the position of offering them advice on another matter down the road.

The Agent's Role

The insurance agent is not just a salesman who's there to try to talk you into a policy with a higher premium. If he's a good agent, he'll be able to explain to you why you need certain coverages and help you figure out the right amounts for your store by preparing a return-on-investment (ROI) estimate. If the agent can't or won't answer your questions, you might be better off looking for another agent – or another insurance carrier. If the insurance company doesn't specialize in your kind of business or the kind of insurance you need, they might not be able to provide the appropriate coverages. Also, do some basic checking on the insurance company at the library or on the Internet. It won't do you much good to have a policy with a carrier that goes bankrupt before they can pay your claim. Insurance companies are rated from A+ to C-, and you'll want to know where yours stands.

The insurance agent doesn't have to be your best friend, but he should be your partner. He's the guy who'll give you the check that helps keep your business going if a disaster should occur, so you want to make sure that you both see eye-to-eye, or at least come to an understanding, about what is appropriate for you and why. Once you're on the same page, you want to be on the agent's radar screen because if you have to file a claim, you want him front and center as soon as possible to help you through the process.

Once you've purchased the policy and are sending in your premiums on a regular basis, your agent should not be a stranger. Although most people would rather do almost anything else, as a good businessperson, you should schedule meetings with the agent two or three times during the year so that you can review your coverage together. Business needs, laws and outside circumstances change often, and you need to ensure that your coverage is sufficient at all times.

Your Obligations as the Insured Party

Obviously, you have to pay your premiums on time, but your responsibilities don't end with writing a check. You have to make the maximum effort to reduce or avoid situations that might lead to the necessity to file insurance claims. That means that you have to adhere to all federal and state laws regarding workplace policies and safety and to take other, reasonable steps to avoid trouble. It is your obligation to keep yourself and your management staff informed of the latest requirements and industry trends. Your insurance agent can also help you stay updated on those things you must do, or not do, and those that it is in your best interest to do, or not do.

You are obligated to conform to OSHA rules, for example, but it also makes sense to keep your walkways clear of snow, ice and debris and to make timely repairs to the building or any fixtures that might pose a danger to a customer or employee.

You also must do your best to avoid doing or not doing something that would lead to your filing an insurance claim, such as accepting a bad check from a known deadbeat, thinking, "I have insurance. The company will cover my loss if the bank doesn't pay." If it can be shown that you knew the check would bounce – because the last sixteen checks the customer wrote all went uncollected, say – the insurance company probably will not pay, and will probably raise your premiums, or even cancel your coverage entirely, to boot. Even if you get away with something marginal, your premiums are likely to go up anyway because you are now considered a higher risk.

Obviously, staging an accident, theft or committing any other type of fraud in order to collect on an insurance policy is illegal and can lead to hefty fines and/or jail time. It goes without saying that it's not worth the risk.

Insurance industry studies have shown that retailers who take proactive steps toward loss prevention have a lower rate of claims – which means that they are experiencing fewer losses than stores that do nothing to combat retail crime. It is a win-win situation for you when you take the proper measures to protect your business.

Situations in Which Your Insurance Company *Won't* Pay

Insurance coverage is extremely complicated, and the complexities are compounded by various jurisdictional requirements. You must know the provisions of your insurance policies inside and out to avoid being hit with a financially devastating surprise.

Many retailers, for example, believe that their general insurance policy covers them for losses due to unknowingly accepting counterfeit cash or checks that bounce. In most cases, however, those retailers would be wrong. You need to have those coverages specifically written into your policy in order to be able to make a claim. If they aren't specified, the business will be stuck holding the bag on the losses. There are special riders that can be purchased, usually for small sums, to cover potential losses that your business might suffer or the needs unique to your industry.

Consider, as an example, standard business property coverages that pertain to losses from counterfeit paper currency or money orders issued by the post office or a bank that are accepted by the store in good faith but are not paid by the issuer. The policy will cover these types of losses up to $1,000; however, if the loss should occur because the store accepts a bogus travelers check or cashier's check, the insurance company won't pay a dime. If you are thoroughly aware of the specifics of your coverage, then you can set sensible store policies to protect the business. In this example, the store might be willing to accept cash and money orders, but not travelers or cashier's checks.

Handling Customer and Employee Insurance Scams

Sometimes people are legitimately injured in a store, and it may be that the business is responsible for the injury because of failure to take an action or correct a condition that led to the person's injury. If this is the case, then the store has no choice but to pay what it owes and take steps to see that the condition is corrected and that it does not occur again in the future.

However, sometimes customers or employees see the store as a "deep-pockets" source of revenue and completely fabricate or greatly exaggerate an injury in order to collect on an insurance claim or a settlement. Some criminals make their living by seeming to shoplift, but in reality, surreptitiously ditching the goods, then allowing themselves to be caught by store security. When the store personnel apprehends a person who does not have the stolen goods, the person can bring a suit against the store – and win monetary damages.

Likewise, people may become injured or claim that they have been injured because of an unsafe condition in your store. Sometimes, these "slip and fall" incidents are brought about because the customer deliberately moves merchandise around in order to create the hazardous condition that precipitates the fall and subsequent injury. Sometimes the falls occur because the store is remiss in not spotting and correcting a dangerous condition that legitimately exists. Either way, the best way to keep injuries down is to inspect the premises on a regular basis and take appropriate corrective action when necessary.

Any time an injury does occur, all witnesses should be asked to write down what they saw, where they were when the accident occurred and the time of the accident. These statements should be completed as soon as possible after the incident, and the witnesses should sign and date their accounts. The documentation should be kept on file. In addition, any tapes from surveillance cameras should be reviewed and retained. If the surveillance equipment shows evidence that the injured party is perpetrating a fraud, that is a powerful argument against making any type of monetary payment.

Not surprisingly, employees as a whole are responsible for the lion's share of business injury claims. Employees are the ones who spend the most time on the premises, so they have the greatest chance of being injured there. However, some employees have figured out that they can go from one company to the next and milk each for a settlement for injuries that supposedly occur on the job. This information can often be uncovered during a pre-employment screening. It has also been demonstrated that during rough economic times, more employees seek disability pay for injuries they claim are sustained on the job, probably because they fear their jobs will be cut, and disability payments guarantee them a steady income. Again, being careful about hiring, proactive about safety, and fanatic about documentation, will be the store's best defenses against spurious workmen's comp claims.

Chapter 11
ARMED ROBBERY

STICK 'EM UP!

Although the fine points will vary according to individual state statutes, robbery is defined as taking something from a person. Armed robbery involves the use of a weapon to do so. According to the Uniform Crime Reports compiled by The U.S. Dept. of Justice, reported incidences of robbery – mostly armed robbery – rose thirty percent in the last decade. During tough economic times, crime in general goes up, and no retailer is immune to armed robbery.

The risks vary depending on the location and type of retail establishment, but it's important for every store to have some overall security rules in place – just in case. Make sure that employees are prepared ahead of time about what to do if they are confronted by a robber, and make sure that you impress upon everyone that common sense is always the rule, especially when you're looking at the wrong end of a weapon.

Keep in mind the consequences of not training everyone: not only do you run the risk of losing more cash or merchandise than you have to, unprepared employees who get hurt – or the families of those who sustain fatal injury – can bring you to financial ruin through expensive litigation. In fact, some laws hold employers responsible for injuries to employees during the course of a violent event such as a robbery. Even if you're not the owner, you may find yourself out of a management job for failing to protect your staff. It's always better to be safe and prepare for something that never happens than to be sorry and wish you had later on.

Proactive Measures

Keep your store windows free of anything that blocks the view of the inside. Exterior obstructions such as tree limbs need to be tended to on a regular basis so that they don't overgrow and get in the way. Interior items such as advertising posters also need to be placed in an unobtrusive manner. An unobstructed view discourages a robber from choosing your shop because it allows passers-by and police to witness interior illegal activity.

Likewise, good lighting around the outside exit doors is important, and those areas should be kept free of bushes and obstacles so that robbers don't have a ready place to hide.

If you invest in closed-circuit surveillance cameras, place them so that they cover areas thieves are likely to target, such as the cash register, safe and displays of valuable merchandise. Cover all entrances and exits as well, especially front and back doors.

Place pieces of tape inside the doors at six-inch intervals (five feet; five feet, six inches; and six feet) to serve as height markers. Carefully measure and clearly label the tape so that if someone flees the store, the height markers can aid in providing a description.

If your store takes in large amounts of money, remove the cash from the drawers at irregular intervals several times during the day. Provide drop safes for cashiers to put bills into between the times that managers empty the registers. Use common sense when counting out cash drawers – don't do it where everyone can see you. Handle money out of sight of the public, such as in the back office. Follow the procedures outlined in Chapter 3 for making bank deposits safely and without attracting attention.

If there is an area of the store that typically has a lot of cash, such as a cashier's cage, you can keep "bait" money within easy reach. In case of a robbery, the employee hands over packets of money that have been seeded with exploding dye devices or with bills whose serial numbers have been recorded.

A bill trap can be set into cash registers. This device sets off a hidden alarm only if the last bill in a drawer is removed during a robbery.

Some stores have adopted a "buddy buzzer" as an alternative to, or in addition to an alarm/security system. An emergency button (a doorbell) is rigged up to ring in an adjoining store. If an incident occurs that requires police response, such as a robbery, the victim presses the buzzer, alerting the neighboring merchant to the need for assistance. When the neighbor arrives, he should *look into* the store first to see what the emergency is. If it is something obvious, such as an armed robbery, the neighboring merchant should leave immediately and alert police. For the buddy buzzer system to work well, it should be hooked up among several neighboring stores.

During the Event

Instruct your employees that, should they be victims of an armed robber, they are to give robbers whatever they demand without arguing or fighting – no one's life or health is worth the cost of merchandise or cash. However, no one should volunteer any information, for example, by saying, "There's more cash in the safe in the back. Do you want me to open it?"

Although everyone's mind will naturally be occupied with thoughts of safety, try to concentrate on memorizing a good description of the robber. Observe the color of hair and eyes, any distinguishing marks or features, clothing and any accent the person might have, as well as a description of any vehicle used. These are the things that will make it easier for police to catch the bad guys.

Also observe anything that the robbers touch. It may help the police get fingerprint evidence.

Try not to antagonize a robber, but remain calm. Refrain from making any sudden movements or shouting. Avoid surprising the robber: if you need to move, say so before doing it.

Afterward

When the robber leaves, do not give chase, but try to note which way he flees and whether he was traveling on foot or in a vehicle. Try to get a description of the car including the plate number, if possible.

Lock the doors immediately, and call the police as soon as it is possible to do so safely. Provide the authorities with as much identifying information about the robbers as you can.

Ask all witnesses, both employees and customers, to write down what happened quickly and without consulting one another. The human memory is notoriously fallible. Sometimes people have false memories about what happened if they have the opportunity to talk about the incident first. The information they provide will be most accurate if it is given individually and as soon as possible.

If you have closed-circuit surveillance cameras in use, provide the tapes to the police.

A lthough the two terms are commonly used interchangeably, burglary is different from robbery. The crime of burglary occurs when an unauthorized person enters the building when it is closed, or hides inside before closing, usually with the intent of stealing.

Peek-a-Boo!

Good interior and exterior lighting discourages nighttime thieves from targeting your shop. Enhance the visibility of the building's exterior by using tamper-resistant lights, such as bulbs enclosed in cages, to illuminate the parking lot as well as any storage sheds or courtyards that may be on your property. Periodically inspect the lights to make sure they are in proper working order.

In addition, provide adequate interior lighting after hours. Keep the front window free of clutter so that passing police can observe any activity going on inside. Assist police in this effort by keeping trees and shrubs trimmed so that they don't block the view, either.

It may sound counter-intuitive at first, but it is also to your advantage to allow potential burglars to see inside your store: if you empty your registers each night and leave the drawers open, would-be thieves can see there is no money to be had without having to break in and damage the registers to find out. Further reduce temptation by keeping cash and any extremely valuable display items locked up in a back-office safe at night.

Although it is generally a good idea to leave the interior view unobstructed, your store may be in an area that demands the use of roll-down gates for protection. These are available in a solid construction, which totally obscures any inside view, or in a construction that is either mostly solid but allows a partial view through a mesh or cage-like area at eye level, or entirely cage-like. With the solid version, potential customers and police alike cannot see into your store. On the other hand, the gates that offer a partial view can also allow vandals access to the window. If defacing of display windows is a problem in your area, you may want to opt for a solid gate. Business district or mall requirements sometimes may dictate the type of gate you will be allowed to use, so be sure to find out before investing in the wrong item.

The Weak Link in the Security Chain

Often, shop owners or property managers go to great pains to ensure that the store's front entrance is protected, then neglect the back door. Leaving the back vulnerable negates the effectiveness of any protection in the front. Often, however, strip mall tenants are at a disadvantage because the standard back door that is provided in many of these properties is simply a hollow metal door, which is easy for burglars to break down or pry open. And although it may be tempting to simply reinforce this type of door with a locking metal crossbar, such a bar presents a danger itself if it is not connected integrally to a panic bar, because it can prevent people from exiting in case of a fire or other disaster. Generally, any locking device that requires "special knowledge or equipment" in order to get the door open, violates basic fire and life safety codes.

Any impediment on the door is a violation when it requires more than one action (such as pushing the panic bar) to exit. In an emergency situation, a non-integrated barrier bar could lead to injury, death and monumental liability for the owner. One way around this danger is to install a device that combines locking at several points – usually the lock and hinge sides and the floor and header sides of the door – with the safety of a paddle exit that provides simultaneous retraction of all dead bolts when pressed.

Ground-level windows should be protected with some sort of grillwork that prevents unauthorized entrance. Both windows and glass doors should be made of a shatter-resistant, or burglar-resistant, material to make it harder for thieves to pull a quick "smash-and-grab" by breaking the glass, reaching inside, stealing whatever merchandise is closest and absconding before the cops arrive.

Other areas of vulnerability include the roof, as well as any trap doors, skylights or other openings that connect to it. Air ducts and ventilation shafts can also provide burglars with a means of entrance to the store. These areas must be closed and locked, and connected to the store's alarm system, if there is one.

Another weak link in the security defense chain is the common walls that are often shared by adjoining businesses in strip malls or other buildings with a large number of tenants or which have undergone renovations. Many times, these walls do not extend to the roof line; rather, they end shortly above the ceiling. The small spaces above these walls are large enough to allow burglars to get into your store – especially if the burglaries originate in the business on the other side of the wall. Work with your neighbors to either extend the walls or block off the spaces using mesh screening or some other appropriate means. If you have an alarm system, let the alarm company know about these areas so that they can install the sensors accordingly.

Moonlight Serenade

Security at the front and back exits, as well as the roof and common walls is a deterrent to unauthorized entrance, and so is an alarm system. Your best bet is an alarm that works through the phone lines to notify the monitoring company and/or police and is backed up through the electrical system in case thieves cut the telephone wires. Many systems are available with 24-hour monitoring and require an access code in order to bypass it to gain entrance. Quality alarms also include a motion detector, smoke detector and a panic button in case of robbery during store hours. The visibility of the system and the loud siren, as well as window stickers provided by the alarm company, act as deterrents to would-be thieves.

Be certain that you know exactly how to activate and deactivate the alarm and that any employee who opens or closes is trained in doing so properly. Most alarms that go off are false, but police have to respond to them anyway. If you tie up law enforcement resources repeatedly with false alarms, many jurisdictions will fine you, hitting you with steadily increasing fines each time a false alarm goes off. A competent alarm installer should be able to install the system so that it's not so sensitive that it goes off at the least gust of wind, but that it works appropriately to pick up motion, heat or light after it is set. Most importantly, remember that an alarm button that notifies police is not to be used for shoplifters or till tappers, or any crime other than robbery.

Before closing at night, confirm that doors are locked securely, not left open a crack or unlocked to allow a would-be thief to return for your merchandise after you go home. Don't just look at the doors, either: pull on them to make sure that a match-book cover or something similar has not been jammed into the door lock, forcing it to remain open. Also, protect yourself from thieves who secrete themselves inside your store before closing by checking out all possible bathrooms, storage areas, closets or crevices where stowaways could hide out until you're gone.

Professional Help

To implement those devices necessary to make your store the most burglar-proof it can be, call on the professionals. Usually, local, city or state police departments make specially-trained officers available to evaluate retail businesses and make recommendations about their security needs. They can tell you about any changes you should make to displays that might afford shoplifters cover, to doors and windows that leave you vulnerable, or anything else they find. They can also point out any weak spots in your store that make you attractive to burglars. This service is also available from consultants or companies that sell security devices, but there may be a fee involved, whereas the local gendarmes typically do the survey gratis.

Chapter 13
PHYSICAL SECURITY

I t's important not to neglect the physical security aspects of your business. You can make all the procedural improvements in the world, but if the building and secure areas within are easy to penetrate, you might as well just hand over the keys to the crooks and tell them to lock up when they're finished cleaning you out.

High-end Systems: Access Control; CCTV, Guards and Alarms

"Access control" is a fancy way of saying "locks" – or a way of regulating who gets to come in and when. Not so long ago, a lock was a mechanical item, requiring a key to open it. Today, traditional locks are still used, of course, but more sophisticated locking mechanisms that rely on computer technology are also available.

Some high-tech access control systems use keypads. The user punches in a specific code – the way you do at an ATM machine, for example – and the entrance unlocks, or not, depending on whether the person's code is functional. With this type of access system, when an employee is terminated or resigns, that person's code is simply deleted from the system, and he cannot enter. Of course, employees can share their codes with one another, the same way they can lend out keys. Many systems will record the information each time the keypad is operated, such as the time and date the entrance was attempted, which door was being accessed, and whether entry was granted, but they can't tell you who punched in the code.

Some keypad systems are connected to alarm systems. A person can open a door with a traditional key, but he must enter the proper code on the keypad inside within a certain number of seconds or an alarm will be sounded and the police or the alarm monitoring company notified.

Another type of access control system is the card-operated lock. The card, which is the size of a credit card, has a magnetic stripe that is coded with information, such as the user's I.D., and areas where that person is allowed to enter, and when. Some systems can be programmed to deny access on the weekends or in the evenings, for example. The user swipes the card through the reader, which records the information about the attempted entry, which is granted or not, depending on whether the person to whom the card is issued has access at that time in that particular place. Again, security can be breached if cards are lent out by employees.

The almost infallible access control system uses biometrics, or some physical characteristic about the person, to identify the user and grant or deny access. Some of the distinctive features that are recognized are fingerprints; voice patterns; hand geometry – recognizing three-dimensional information about a person's hand; and retinal scanning – reading the characteristics about the retina in the back of the eye. The user can also be assigned a verification card that is swiped or otherwise presented, and that entry card together with the biometric recognition, tells the system whether that person should be allowed in.

Naturally, the more sophisticated the system, the more it costs. Keypad and card-swipe access control systems are typical in a retail establishment, while biometrics are generally used in extremely secure facilities, such as nuclear power plants.

Closed-circuit television, or CCTV, systems, provide good security both inside the store as well as in outside areas, such as parking lots and loading docks. Improvements in CCTV systems are keeping pace with the developments in broadcast media. Digital cameras are available, and color systems can be used instead of black-and-white. CCTV cameras can tilt, zoom and pan. The systems can record continuously, or they can take still shots every few seconds.

One person can keep tabs on several different areas of the store by watching a bank of video monitors at one time, which reduces the number of personnel needed to keep the store under surveillance. The drawback to watching monitors is that many people tend to get bored after a time and look away, so they might miss something. Rotating the personnel who watch the monitors every couple of hours helps reduce the risk that they will fail to see something important occurring on camera. Videotapes can also be kept as a record and reviewed later on if something needs to be looked at again.

CCTV cameras are helpful when used to monitor the goings-on in vulnerable areas, such as parts of the store where high-ticket merchandise is displayed, stockrooms, and cash registers.

Surveillance can be coupled with deterrence by posting uniformed security guards near the exits and having undercover "floorwalkers" circulate among the customers to observe whether any thefts are taking place.

The visible security officer may deter amateur shoplifters and kids, but probably will not discourage professionals. Whether you contract with an agency to supply security guards or the loss prevention officers are on the store's payroll, bear in mind that the store owner is responsible for their behavior. Courteous, helpful security personnel enhances the store's image; disheveled guards or those who do not follow the rules send customers away, and in the worst case, can get the store sued for inappropriate behavior, such as making apprehensions improperly.

Security officers are an expense, but if you're paying for them to be there, they should be allowed to do their jobs and not asked to fill in for maintenance personnel, loading dock employees, or in other non-security functions. By taking them off their posts and having them perform tasks unrelated to security, you dilute their power of deterrence.

Also, don't allow employees to fall into the trap of thinking that they're off the hook just because there's a security guard around. *Security Is Everybody's Business*, and personnel should not be lulled into a sense of complacency about their role in the overall crime prevention strategy of the store.

Another security consideration is an alarm system. There are several types of systems that perform different functions. Each type comes in various price ranges. There is also the option of leasing the system or buying it outright, which will also affect the cost.

Alarm sensors are connected to potential points of entry, such as doors and windows. Once the alarm is activated, if the connection is interfered with by, say, an intruder opening a door, a signal goes out. Some alarms make noise, setting off sirens and activating lights. Others are silent, automatically dialing the police or the alarm monitoring company without alerting the intruder. Some both make noise and send out a telephonic signal.

The flashing lights and blaring siren may scare off an intruder and can attract the attention of neighbors who may call the police in response to the disturbance.

The silent alarm sends a signal through the telephone lines to let the cops or the alarm company know that the alarm security has been breached. Some of the automatic dialing alarms have cellular back-up in case a burglar cuts the telephone lines.

Alarm systems also come with features that will alert the fire department in case of a fire, or with a hold-up button that is placed in a discreet place, such as under the counter. If it is pressed, the alarm company will notify the police of a robbery in progress, without store personnel having to perform an overt act and thus alerting the robber that help is being summoned.

There are many combinations and functions of alarm systems, so you should shop around for the most suitable equipment for your store's needs. Ask the local police department to do a walk-through of your store and point out the areas of vulnerability so that you can address them with the alarm company representative. Get advice from other local merchants, too. Check with other tenants in your mall or local area, and canvass your competitors about the types of systems that they use.

Another decision that needs to be made is whether to purchase the alarm equipment outright or to lease it. When you purchase the system, you then have to pay either the company that installed it or an independent firm for monitoring services. Also, technology changes quickly, and you may be stuck with old equipment after it has outlived its usefulness. On the other hand, if you lease, you may pay next to nothing for the equipment itself, but you may be locked into a long-term contract with fees that escalate annually.

Be sure to ask questions of the sales representative, check references, and speak with other retailers before signing on the dotted line.

Low-end: Locks, Safes, the "Doorbell"

Mechanical locks come in many varieties, and some are more effective than others. The single biggest breach of lock security, however, is failure to limit the number of keys that are issued. The locks can be top of the line, but if too many keys are floating around unaccounted for, sooner or later one of them will find its way into the hands of someone not authorized to use it. Issue keys on a "need-access only" basis, and carefully document who receives which keys. Be sure to collect keys from any employees who leave the company. If you aren't able to get the keys back, then change the locks. It's also not a wise idea to have a lot of master keys floating around. A master key will open many different locks, so the more people who have one, the more chances there are of security breaches occurring.

Unauthorized key duplication is another concern. One way to limit it is to use high-security locks whose keys cannot be made by just any locksmith. High-security key blanks are carefully controlled by the manufacturer and distributor. Stamping a key that is easy to copy, "Do

Not Duplicate" hardly ever deters people from having reproductions made.

A safe is a, well, safe place to keep valuables, such as cash and blank checks. There are two varieties of safes: the kind that resists fire and the type that is meant to resist break-ins. Most safes are designed to perform one or the other function; usually, they do not do both. Assess your needs to determine which type you require.

Whichever kind of safe you decide on, make sure that it is large and heavy – not something portable that anyone could walk off with. Preferably, it should be fastened to the floor or some other part of the building structure. Safes can be connected to the alarm system, and a motion detector can also be used to determine whether someone is around it when they shouldn't be.

Security experts are divided about whether a safe is best kept hidden or exposed. If it is near a window or door, anyone who attempts to tamper with it will be seen easily. If it is kept hidden, it does not provide temptation to would-be thieves, but it does give someone who wants to break into it the opportunity to do so without an audience.

One way to enhance your store's security is by using a primitive doorbell system, or "buddy buzzer," that connects to an adjoining shop. If a robber should enter your store, the person at the front counter can press the buzzer, which is hidden under the counter. It sounds in your next-door neighbor's store, alerting him that something is going on in your establishment. Your merchant buddy can then take a peek into your store to determine whether you have an emergency, and call the police if necessary.

You will also have a doorbell connection that will alert you if something happens in your neighbor's store. By setting up this kind of alarm signal, shopkeepers can look out for each other.

Outside Protection: Fences, Windows, Motion Detectors

In security circles, the outside, or perimeter, of your building is called the primary zone of protection. Simply put, your first line of physical protection begins well outside the building. In some locales, where stores are freestanding, this means that you will want, or be required by local statute, to put up fencing. In mall situations or more crowded urban areas, it may be a question of using pull-down security gates.

In many situations, you will have to put up the type of fencing that your jurisdiction or lease requires. Should you have more freedom of choice in the matter, your decision about the type and placement of fencing will take into consideration aesthetics as well as functionality. As an example, you could put up electrified fencing with rolls of concertina wire on the top, which might deter shoplifters, but it wouldn't be very welcoming to potential customers. Your neighbors might also complain about the unsightliness. Common sense often dictates that you go with a tasteful wooden or chain-link fence.

If your perimeter dictates the installation of a pull-down security gate rather than a fence, you will need to know whether a certain type is required or whether the decision is left to you. Some pull-down gates are solid, allowing passers-by a view of the windows or interior of your store. Others have a small grated opening through which a sliver of a view is allowed, and still others are completely grated, allowing full view.

The disadvantages of using a gate with any kind of opening is that vandals can reach inside and deface the windows or doors with paint or by scratching or breaking the glass. If your store is in an area where this type of crime is commonplace, it may make sense for you to use a solid gate. On the other hand, by using a gate that is completely or partially open, you can maximize your merchandising by allowing window shoppers to do just that, and perhaps your displays will entice them to return during business hours. An opening in the gate also allows police and other passers-by to look inside your store, so that if an intruder is inside after hours, he can be spotted from outside. With a solid gate, no one can see what's going on once the gate is pulled down.

Keep in mind that, as with other aspects of security, you must balance protection with buyer appeal. It is always a fine line to walk, and you may very well be nudged in one direction or another by lease provisions or local laws. Again, it is worthwhile to ask local law enforcement, mall security, fellow tenants and competitors for the benefit of their experience in these matters.

Over half of all break-ins occur through windows, so their protection needs special consideration. Security experts agree that any opening that is larger than 96 square inches and less than 18 feet from the ground poses a security risk and needs to be protected. For windows that open, a locking device such as a slide bar, crossbar with padlock, or bolt should be used to secure them from the inside. Windows in the rear of a building can be covered with bars that are installed with security screws – special screws that require the use of a special type of screwdriver, rather than one any thief can pick up in a hardware store.

If there are a lot of concerns in your area about intruders gaining entry through front windows, decorative iron grillwork (bars) may be an aesthetically pleasing as well as functional balance. However, keep in mind that covering windows with bars or grills may pose a risk to persons inside the store should a fire occur.

Another method of window protection is the use of security glazing, or security glass. Security glass – which may be glass or a glass synthetic – is resistant to flame, heat, cold, and implements such as hammers and picks, as well as rocks. While it can crack, it is almost impossible to breach. Security film can also be used. It is placed on the window itself and prevents someone from smashing the glass in order to gain entry or to pull a "smash-and-grab" type theft of merchandise that is just inside a window. The security film is see-through, so it does not defeat the purpose of a display window.

Windows can be further protected through the use of contacts that pick up the motion of the window being opened. Glass-break detectors can also be installed. Should the window glass be broken, these devices will be activated by the vibration and sound. Both of these devices are incorporated into the alarm system. Of course, the more bells and whistles your alarm system has, the more it will cost. Security costs and risks have to be weighed to determine the right combination for your store.

The Back Door: Combine Safety with Fire Protection Compliance

While a front door may have to be glass in order to conform to the appearance in the rest of a mall or strip center, it is desirable to have a see-through entrance door that is inviting to potential customers.

The back door, however, is a different story. Often, the rear entrances to mall or strip mall stores are the weakest link in the security chain. Pay careful attention to the type of door and installation you have in the back, and if it is not adequate, discuss the possibility of making changes with the lessor. It may cost you some money to modify the back door, but it will be worth it to have the proper protection in place.

Doors are vulnerable to unauthorized entry at the lock, frame, hinges and panels. After making sure that you have a good, pick-resistant lock in place, consider the construction of the door frame next. It should be heavy enough that someone wielding a crowbar cannot gain entry. Solid wood, a minimum of two inches thick, is recommended for both frame and panels.

Hinges should be located on the inside, rather than the outside, of the door, so that they are not so vulnerable to would-be intruders. Pins should be welded, rather than removable.

Glass doors should be constructed of safety glass, just as windows are. Security grills help protect them after-hours.

All doors should be monitored by the alarm system, and a minimum of 60 watts of illumination should be placed above each door.

In old buildings, some doors have transoms, or window-like openings above the doors. If you have a transom that can be sealed without compromising ventilation, you should do so. If you must be able to open the transom, it can be fitted with locks. It should be kept locked when no one is in the building.

Back doors should be kept locked at all times. However, fire codes generally prohibit emergency-exit doors from being secured in such a way that a person attempting to exit must have "special knowledge or equipment" to do so. In other words, you can't have an emergency-exit door that can be opened from the inside only with a key, or that is secured with a chain and padlock. Instead, doors should be equipped with a panic bar, or crash bar, which needs only to be pushed in order for the door to open. The emergency-exit device can be hooked up to the alarm system so that if someone hides inside the store and tries to leave through the emergency door after hours, the alarm sounds or the monitoring company is notified. These devices can be turned off with a key to allow legitimate egress.

Up Above: The Roof

Another point of vulnerability that many people don't think about is the roof. Like the back door, the roof is not often built in the most secure fashion. Also, typically, nobody can see what's happening on the roof, which gives the bad guys almost unlimited time to break in or work their way in through skylights or ventilation ducts. If there are openings on the roof, secure them from inside with grating or bars to make it harder for thieves to sneak in, and connect them to the alarm system.

Unauthorized access from the roof is even easier in strip malls or other settings where building roofs are connected. If local regulations allow it, a chain-link fence topped with barbed wire can deter roof entries.

Like the roof, common walls and floors also provide an opportunity for unauthorized entry. If your neighbor's roof is vulnerable and an intruder breaks in from above, or if someone hides in your neighbor's establishment and waits until after closing, he can take his time to work his way into your store via the floor or wall. It is in your best interest to speak with the landlord and your neighbors to ensure that everyone's buildings are properly secured.

A Gun for Protection: the Pros and Cons

Many people who keep illegal firearms on the their premises for protection purposes believe that "it's better to be tried by twelve than carried by six." In other words, they're willing to risk the legal penalties for having a gun or using one improperly in order to safeguard themselves and their property.

Whether your personal philosophy is in line with this manner of thinking or not, there are aspects to gun ownership that must be seriously considered.

First of all, if you own a gun, you must be proficient in its use. That may mean signing up for classes and practicing firing it regularly. If you don't know what you're doing or are out of practice, you take the risk that when you use it against a bad guy, you may harm innocent people. Learning and practicing with your gun will require an investment of time and money.

The prevailing philosophy of gun use is that if you pick up a firearm, you must be prepared to kill someone with it. Taking a life is a very serious matter that is likely to have lasting effects on the person who does so. It is very difficult for even a skilled marksman to just "wing" a person by shooting him in the arm or leg. If you're in the midst of a robbery, you are not likely to be calm and cool, and your chances of being able to aim properly are almost nil. Also, consider that a bullet that enters any part of a person's body – not just the heart or head, say – can be fatal. You also take the risk of shooting an innocent bystander. Most robbers don't stand still and provide a perfect target for the shooter; they're constantly in motion.

If someone is pulling an armed robbery, he is not likely to be calm, either. He may be very twitchy and nervous. If he sees that you have a gun, the situation is likely to escalate quickly. He may shoot you before you get a chance to aim at him. Is it worth your life to protect some merchandise?

Also, don't overlook the seriousness of breaking laws while using a firearm. The statutes vary from jurisdiction to jurisdiction, even within the same state, so you must familiarize yourself with the prevailing laws. Even if you are legally entitled to own a gun, you often are prohibited from using it during the very situations you thought you could. You can't shoot a bad guy while he's fleeing, for example, and you probably aren't allowed to shoot someone in order to protect mere property, no matter what its dollar value is. Don't underestimate the legal jeopardy you could put yourself into by violating a gun law: you may think you're just protecting yourself, but a judge may see it differently and send you to prison. It has happened before, and it is likely to happen again. Are you willing to gamble that it won't happen to you?

If you familiarize yourself with the laws regarding firearms, become proficient with your gun, and decide that you can live with whatever consequences may befall you as a result of using it, then you must have a safety plan in place. The gun should be kept hidden and out of reach of any minors. Some security experts recommend keeping it in a back room because robbers often take their victims to a back room to search for money. You will have to have it in a place where nosy employees won't find it, but that is within easy access should you be forced at gunpoint into the room.

All in all, the decision to keep a gun is fraught with pitfalls. Be sure you are thoroughly aware of the risks, and balance them against what you might hope to gain by having a firearm.

Chapter 14
WORKPLACE VIOLENCE

Workplace violence is an important safety and health issue in today's workplace. Its most extreme form, homicide, is the third leading cause of fatal occupational injury in the United States. According to the Bureau of Labor Statistics (BLS) Census of Fatal Occupational Injuries (CFOI), there were 674 workplace homicides in 2000, accounting for 11 percent of the total 5,915 fatal work injuries in the United States. Interestingly enough, figures show that the highest number of non-fatal violent incidents in the workplace aren't in construction or agriculture or mining – they're in the retail trade and service industries.

The Occupational Safety and Health Administration (OSHA) has developed guidelines and recommendations to reduce worker exposures to the hazard of workplace violence, but the issue is confusing because its definition is broad, and it varies depending on who's discussing it. It can include everything from a frustrated employee slamming his fist on his desk to murder, and everything in between. What's most important for a store owner or manager to know is that you must understand the risks and implement a policy to reduce the chances that violence will occur in your workplace.

Not doing so can lead to monetary losses from a number of directions: lost productivity, workman's compensation payments for injured employees, possible punitive damages imposed by the court because of your failure to ensure the safety of your employees, and many more.

Going Postal: Could it Happen in Your Store?

"Going postal" is a colorful term that was coined when the media reported incidences of postal workers who went on shooting rampages. Every retailer needs to realize that workplace violence is not limited to letter carriers – and it's not something that happens only to "the other guy." It's a very real threat in *your* store, to *your* employees.

In the United States between 1993 and 1999, 18 percent of violent crimes were committed while the victim was working or on duty – a rate of 13 per 1,000 persons in the workforce. The acts of non-fatal violence that were perpetrated included rape and sexual assault, robbery, aggravated assault, and simple assault. As of 1997, statistics show that 20 workers are murdered each week, and 18,000 per week are victims of nonfatal workplace assaults.

A hostile workplace presents safety and health concerns on several levels, ranging from a lack of training and safety information to physical assault. Distractions while working can lead to not taking proper safety precautions, resulting in on-the-job injuries. The effects of a hostile workplace can be reflected in acute as well as chronic stress reactions, and OSHA has begun to recognize workplace violence as an occupational safety and health issue.

Combative and Violent Customers

Homicide is the second leading cause of death on the job, and the leading cause of workplace death among females and workers under 18 years of age. The majority of workplace homicides are robbery-related crimes committed by persons unknown to the victims, and about three-quarters of these homicides are committed with a firearm.

Factors that place workers at risk for violence in the workplace include interacting with the public, exchanging money, delivering services or goods, working late at night or during early morning hours, working alone, guarding valuable goods or property, and dealing with violent people or volatile situations – many of which are conditions present in retail businesses.

The person who is deranged, drug-addicted or violent for some other reason, usually comes into a retail establishment for the purpose of committing a crime there. Following the safety guidelines throughout this book will help reduce the risk of an occurrence of workplace violence in a given situation.

OSHA's recommended guidelines for engineering and administrative controls

◆ Physical barriers such as bullet-resistant enclosures or shields, pass-through windows, or deep service counters

◆ Alarm systems, panic buttons, global positioning systems (GPS), and radios ("open mike switch")

◆ Convex mirrors, elevated vantage points, clear visibility of service and cash register areas

◆ Bright and effective lighting

◆ Adequate staffing

◆ Arrange furniture to prevent entrapment

◆ Cash-handling controls, use of drop safes

◆ Height markers on exit doors

◆ Emergency procedures to use in case of robbery

◆ Training in identifying hazardous situations and appropriate responses in emergencies

◆ Video surveillance equipment, in-car surveillance cameras, and closed circuit TV

◆ Establish liaison with local police

The Employee Victim: Domestic Violence Spillover

An employee who is a victim of domestic violence may be perceived as a problem to the business because of time off due to injuries or court cases, or a decrease in productivity or effectiveness. But a domestic violence victim poses another problem to the business as well: there is a chance that the perpetrator will follow the victim onto the store premises and commit a violent act in the workplace. This kind of a problem is not just the victim's problem – it's yours, as well. As an employer or manager, you have an obligation to protect employees against workplace violence, regardless of the source.

Follow all established safety procedures to reduce the risk of violence from any source. If you become aware that an employee is having a problem of this nature, let the worker know that you will help protect her or him. That means that if the victim has an order of protection or restraining order that prohibits the abuser from coming into contact with her or him, personnel stationed at the door, such as greeters or security guards should be made aware that the perpetrator is not to enter the premises. You must do whatever is necessary to protect employees against violence, regardless of its source.

And remember – women are not the only victims of domestic violence. Men also suffer from this problem.

Employee-on-Employee Violence

Violence can erupt in the workplace spontaneously; it can build up over time; or it can occur because an employee returns to wreak havoc after being fired.

As part of sensible safety measures, roughhousing should be prohibited. This kind of "innocent" horseplay can mask aggressive tendencies and can lead to more serious incidences of violence. Employees who violate the rules should be disciplined.

If a worker has a beef with a colleague or supervisor, it could lead to a violent act. Managers and supervisors should make it their business to detect these kinds of difficulties and defuse the situation immediately. Good management techniques call for recognizing each employee's customary behavior anyway, so any resentments should become obvious quickly.

The terminated employee who returns to the workplace with a firearm or other weapon in order to retaliate for being fired or mistreated has probably come to the attention of management several times previously. Prior to the exit interview with the problem employee, it may be a good idea to consult with an employment counselor. You may be able to arrange for the counselor to meet with the terminated individual immediately after the firing. These counselors, who are employees of outside placement firms, are valuable because they can act as sounding boards for the individual's frustrations. They can also help direct the worker's energies into a positive direction, such as exploring training opportunities or job interviewing workshops that might be available.

Regardless of whether anyone is available to meet with a dismissed employee afterward, any locks to which the person has had access during his tenure should be changed, as should alarm codes. Employee identification and any company charge cards must also be returned by the person at the time of the termination. It should be a strongly enforced company policy that no one be allowed entrance without displaying the proper credentials. An employee who is terminated on a security guard's day off could return to wreak havoc in a secure area of the store because the guard didn't know the person was no longer working in the store and failed to check for identification, for example.

The Obligation to Keep Employees Safe

OSHA does not have a specific standard for workplace violence. However, under the Occupational Safety and Health Act of 1970, the extent of an employer's obligation to address workplace violence is governed by the General Duty Clause:

Section 5(a)(1) of the OSH Act, or P.L. 91-596 (the "General Duty Clause") provides that "Each employer shall furnish to each of his employees employment and a place of employment which are free from recognized hazards that are causing or are likely to cause death or serious physical harm to his employees." 29 U.S.C. 654(a)(1)

It is, therefore, OSHA's commitment to encourage employers to develop workplace violence prevention programs. OSHA's Sample Workplace Violence Prevention Program can be found in Appendix A, but some of OSHA's recommendations are as follows:

- **Management commitment and employee involvement.** May include simply clear goals for worker security in smaller sites or a written program for larger organizations.

- **Worksite analysis.** Involves identifying high-risk situations through employee surveys, workplace walkthroughs, and reviews of injury/illness data.

- **Hazard prevention and control.** Calls for designing engineering and administrative and work practice controls to prevent or limit violent incidents.

- **Training and education.** Ensures that employees know about potential security hazards and ways to protect themselves and their co-workers.

Post-incident response and evaluation are essential to an effective violence prevention program. All workplace violence programs should provide treatment for victimized employees and employees who may be traumatized by witnessing a workplace violence incident. Several types of assistance can be incorporated into the post-incident response, including trauma-crisis counseling, critical incident stress debriefing, or employee assistance programs to assist victims.

Chapter 15
SEXUAL HARASSMENT

S exual harassment is increasingly being recognized as a safety and health issue, not just a minor annoyance or a figment of some overly sensitive employee's imagination. Sexual harassment also violates laws prohibiting sex discrimination in employment. It is an issue that must be dealt with, or, as with many problems, the outcome could be financially disastrous for the store should an affected employee bring a lawsuit for failing to prevent or stop the harassment.

Establish a policy, state the consequences for violating it – and stick to it.

A Definition of Sexual Harassment

Under Title VII of the Civil Rights Act of 1964, as amended, unwelcome sexual advances, requests for sexual favors, and other verbal or physical conduct of a sexual nature constitutes sexual harassment when

◆ submission to such conduct is made, either explicitly or implicitly, a term or condition of an individual's employment;
◆ submission to, or rejection of, such conduct by an individual is used as the basis for employment decisions affecting such individual; or
◆ such conduct has the purpose or effect of unreasonably interfering with an individual's work performance or creating an intimidating, hostile, or offensive working environment.

While the problem of sexual harassment is gaining increased attention in all workplaces and civil rights remedies are more aggressively pursued, many are beginning to see it not only as an issue of employment discrimination but as a real workplace safety and health issue as well. The International Labour Organization, the Trades Union Council, and the Canadian Labour Congress have publicly recognized sexual harassment as an important health and safety issue. There is growing evidence that sexual harassment, at a minimum, is a stress producer and, in its more extreme forms, can pose a danger as a result of distraction, fear, and assault.

Some forms of sexual harassment include, but are not limited to

◆ uninvited sexually suggestive looks, comments, joking, or gestures from supervisors or co-workers

◆ subtle forms of sexual harassment such as being stared at, "pinups" of naked and nearly naked women, and unwanted sexual remarks (including comments on appearance)

◆ being touched in sexual ways

◆ sexual assault

◆ co-workers who spread vile rumors, or playing "pranks" such as putting condoms on the victims' car antennas

◆ unwanted physical contact, including that of a sexual nature, from co-workers and/or supervisors

---

Who's Affected

Sexual harassment in the workplace is an equal employment opportunity issue. Both men and women can be sexually harassed by persons of either gender.

Men are sometimes more reluctant to report being sexually harassed because doing so may be contrary to their images of themselves as "macho" or "in control." It is especially important, therefore, to treat every employee who reports sexual harassment with dignity and to take each complaint seriously.

Put it in Writing

It is necessary to have written policy in place that states prohibited behavior and the consequences to the employee who engages in it. This policy must be enforced across the board.

A sexual harassment policy can be modeled after the one in Appendix B.

Avoid Taking the Heat for Employee Actions

Recent Supreme Court rulings have expanded employer liability for the actions of employees, so establishing a policy and sticking to it is of utmost importance in order to protect the business against lawsuits.

Regarding sexual harassment in the workplace, the "reasonable care" standard applies.

To defend themselves, employers would have to show that they exercise reasonable care to prevent, or promptly correct, any sexually harassing behavior.
                                                — Federal Supreme Court, 1998

"Reasonable care" means that the employer could be liable for sexual harassment damages even if

◆ the victim never complained to the company

◆ the harasser is a coworker, not a supervisor

◆ the harasser is a customer

◆ the harasser and the victim are the same sex

◆ the investigating supervisor did not pursue the investigation out of respect for the victim's request for confidentiality

◆ the victim perceives his or her own opportunities impeded by a manager's sexual harassment of, or legitimate consensual relationship with, another employee

Chapter 16
WORKPLACE SAFETY

 mployers have both a moral and a legal obligation to protect workers. To do so properly, businesses must comply with the health and safety standards and requirements which are set by federal, state and local laws.

One of the most important agencies to know about is the Occupational Safety and Health Administration (OSHA). OSHA was created in 1971 to prevent work-related injuries, illnesses, and deaths. Since its inception, occupational deaths have been cut in half and injuries have declined by 40 percent. However, there are still a staggering number of work-related injuries, illnesses, and deaths each year. In 1999, for example, there were 5.7 million occupational injuries and illnesses among U.S. workers. Almost 7 out of every 100 workers experienced a job-related injury or illness, and 6,023 workers lost their lives on the job.

OSHA Compliance

OSHA sets standards that employers are required to meet. It is your responsibility to familiarize yourself with the ones that apply to your business and to comply with them. Failure to do so can result in being assessed with penalties up to $70,000, depending upon how likely the violation is to result in serious harm to workers.

You can access the information you need from the OSHA Web site at www.osha.gov. The agency also makes "The OSHA Handbook for Small Businesses" available to employers and managers to help them meet OSHA's legal requirements. You can download this handbook free from the Web site at http://www.osha-slc.gov/Publications/osha2209.pdf.

In addition, all employers must post the federal or a state OSHA poster in the workplace in order to provide their employees with information on their safety and health rights. You can order a printed copy from the OSHA Publications Office by calling (800) 321-OSHA, or you can download one from the Internet and print it out from the Web site at www.osha-slc.gov/pls/publications/pubindex.list#3165. You can also get a poster in Spanish from the Web site.

Employer Obligations

You are required to know the laws and rules that affect your business and to comply with them. One of the trickiest areas these days has to do with smoking in the workplace. The rules and laws are changing rapidly, but you must keep up with them or risk being fined or penalized in other ways.

You must also communicate the safety rules and regulations to all employees and ensure that everyone follows the established procedures. It is best to incorporate your safety rules and/or worksheet with the company's other policies in the employee handbook.

If there are hazards present in the workplace, you may be able to get help from OSHA to fix them. You can contact the OSHA Consultation Program for your state for free on-site assistance in identifying and correcting hazards or setting up safety and health programs. You can also contact the OSHA Area Office nearest you to speak to the compliance assistance specialist about training and education in job safety and health issues. Another option is OSHA Advisors, interactive software that "walks" you through specific OSHA standards or helps identify potential hazards throughout your workplace.

OSHA will also help you get workplace safety and health training. Contact the nearest OSHA Area Office and speak with the compliance assistance specialist. You also can check out training that is available at the OSHA Training Institute in the Chicago area, or at one of the 20 education centers located at colleges and universities around the nation.

SAMPLE HEALTH AND SAFETY PROGRAM FOR RETAIL SMALL BUSINESS

Use this sample as a guideline to help you prepare your written health and safety program.

This is only a guideline. You'll need to tailor it to meet the health and safety needs of your particular workplace. For example, you'll need to add specific information on written safe work **procedures, state any personal protective equipment you need, list additional training and orientation topics, and provide details about first aid and emergency procedures.**

HEALTH AND SAFETY POLICY

(Name of firm) _____ wants its workplace to be a healthy and safe environment. To achieve this, our firm will establish and maintain an occupational health and safety program designed to prevent injuries and disease. The employer is responsible for providing workers with adequate instruction in health and safety and for addressing unsafe situations in a timely, effective manner. All workers and service contractors are required to work safely and to know and follow our company guidelines for safe work procedures.

Signed _____ Date _____

Employer's responsibilities include

- Establishing the health and safety program
- Conducting and annual review in (month) of each year
- Training supervisors
- Providing a safe and healthy work environment

Supervisors' responsibilities include

- Orienting new workers
- Ongoing training of workers
- Conducting regular staff safety meetings

- Performing inspections and investigations
- Reporting any safety or health hazards
- Correcting unsafe acts and conditions

Workers, responsibilities include

- Learning and following safe work procedures
- Correcting hazards or reporting them to supervisors
- Participating in inspections and investigations where applicable
- Using personal protective equipment where required
- Helping to create a safe workplace by recommending ways to improve the health and safety program

WRITTEN SAFE WORK PROCEDURES

(You need to have written procedures for high-risk or complex tasks. List these high-risk tasks here. A WCB safety or hygiene officer may be able to advise you on procedures you need to include. For example, you may need written safe work procedures for using special equipment, dealing with shoplifters, or working alone. Attach the procedures to this program.)

PERSONAL PROTECTIVE EQUIPMENT (PPE)

(List any PPE required, when it must be used, and where it can be found. For example, workers may be required to wear eye protection when using certain equipment. Attach this list to this program.)

EDUCATION AND TRAINING

All workers will be given an orientation by their supervisor immediately upon hiring. The following topics will be included in the orientation:

- Fire exit routes and marshaling area
- Location of first aid kit and fire extinguisher
- How to report accidents and injuries
- Location of material safety data sheets (MSDSs). (MSDSs are provided by suppliers of chemical products and contain information on how to handle

and use the chemical product safely.)
- Workplace Hazardous Materials Information System (WHMIS) training for any hazardous product in the workplace
- Applicable written procedures

The employer will make sure that staff receive further training when necessary to ensure the safe performance of their duties. Staff meetings are one way to increase safety awareness.

(For higher hazard work areas and jobs, orientation in additional topics may be necessary. List these topics here.)

_____

_____

INSPECTIONS

A supervisor and a worker will conduct regular inspections to identify hazards and recommend how to eliminate or minimize the hazards. The inspection will also look at how work is performed.

Serious hazards or unsafe work practices discovered during inspections or observed by workers, supervisors, or the employer will be dealt with immediately. Other hazards will be dealt with as soon as possible.

(State how often inspections will be performed — typically once a month or at other intervals that prevent the development of unsafe working conditions. It's useful to inspect the workplace before a staff meeting so results can be discussed with staff.)

HAZARDOUS MATERIALS AND SUBSTANCES

(If you use hazardous materials or substances at your workplace, list them here. Also list the location of material safety data sheets [MSDSs], and any applicable written work procedures.)

_____

FIRST AID

This workplace keeps a _(type)_____ first aid kit in the _(location)_____ . *(Give the name of your first aid attendant if one is required. Also provide ambulance and hospital phone numbers.)*

_____

EMERGENCY PREPAREDNESS

Fire — See the fire plan posted at _(location)_____ .

Fire extinguishers are located at (list locations):

_____

(Names of employees) _____

_____ are trained to use them.

Earthquake — An annual inspection will be conducted, focusing on objects that may pose a hazard during an earthquake. The exit and marshaling procedures are the same as for fires. *(Or, if not, note the location of earthquake procedures here.)* _____

(Note other emergency procedures, such as protection from violence.)

_____

INVESTIGATING ACCIDENTS

A supervisor and a worker must investigate any injuries or close calls on the same day the incident occurs. Any incident that results in an injury requiring medical treatment, or that had the potential for causing serious injury, must be investigated immediately. The purpose of an investigation is to find out what went wrong, determine whether our health and safety practices were faulty, and most importantly, recommend actions that will prevent a recurrence of the problem.

RECORDS AND STATISTICS

Accurate health and safety records provide an excellent gauge to determine how we are doing. The following records are maintained and will be reviewed annually:

- Claims statistics
- First aid records
- Completed inspection lists

- Occurrence investigations
- Material safety data sheets
- Any WCB inspection reports

These records are kept at _(location)_____ .

Medically related records will be handled in a manner that respects confidentiality.

Courtesy Workers' Compensation Board of British Columbia, Canada (WCB) www.worksafebc.com

Chapter 17
DOING BUSINESS ON THE INTERNET

L et's face it: the Internet isn't the wave of the future; it's the reality of the present. Whether you love it or hate it, you might as well get used to the idea that more and more shopping is being done online. Retailers who want to remain competitive will have to figure out a way to establish an Internet presence.

Putting your business on the Internet can be done in ways that range from simple to extremely complex. How you set up your Web presence depends on what you want to realize from it.

Is your goal to provide basic information about your store, such as location, telephone numbers and hours of operation so that Web surfers can find you easily? Or do you want to put your entire inventory on your Web site and sell both online and in a brick-and-mortar setting? Or perhaps you want to strike a balance, offering a few products or services online, but keeping the Web site simple and easy to manage.

If you aren't sure what you want to do, start by surfing the Web yourself to see what competitors are doing. You can find other businesses like yours through search engines such as Google or through links from industry Web sites.

Once you get a handle on your competition, you may find it useful to discuss your goals with a Web designer. Don't know where to find one? Take a look at the bottom of the home page of a Web site you like. Many Web masters have links to their own sites, where you can view online portfolios. E-mail a designer or two, request a proposal, and compare prices.

If all you want to do is have a basic site that lists some information – sort of like an online Yellow Pages ad – you can consider using a site that gives you free hosting and allows you to build your own site. Keep in mind that you probably won't be able to make any direct sales through a free site.

If you do decide to take the plunge and sell on the Net, you will need to be aware of the risk that you or your customers may become victims of cyber-crime and develop a plan to safeguard yourself as well as your buyers.

Because of the rapid changes in technology and rules regarding the Internet, you must constantly stay on top of everything related to cyber-selling. The information presented here is only a general guideline.

Protect Your Business Against Cyber-Crime

A simple and pretty safe way to get started is by listing your products through an online auction site, such as eBay or Amazon.com. These sites allow you to sell your products through them in exchange for a fee or a percentage of the sale price.

Some sites handle the money collection for you, so all you have to do is ship out the product and have the profits deposited directly into your bank account. If you use this type of site, both your financial information and that of your buyers is kept confidential by the auction site, so there's no risk to either party. Many sites also have a guarantee that protects buyers and sellers. The large, well-known sites that operate like this must be trustworthy, or they wouldn't be able to stay in business.

With other types of auction or sale sites, you have to make the payment arrangements directly with the buyers for each item you sell. If you don't want to wait for someone to send you a check, you can use a service like PayPal, which acts as an intermediary by collecting the money from the buyer for you in exchange for a small percentage of the amount of sale. Once you receive electronic confirmation that PayPal has received the funds, you can electronically deposit the money into your account. You don't get the buyer's account information, and the buyer doesn't get yours, so it's generally a very safe way to conduct business.

However, if you go the more in-depth route of setting up an inventory listing and a direct payment method on your own site, it becomes more complicated. Be sure that you work with a Web designer who has experience with setting up electronic shopping carts. Also, you'll need to figure out how you will accept payments from customers.

Most people who shop online use credit cards, so you will want to be able to accommodate them in order to maximize sales. If you already accept credit cards, check with the bank or company that processes your transaction to find out whether they offer online services as well as point-of-sale services.

Once you have everything in place, make sure to keep yourself abreast of all the changes to the rules for Internet sales. Your bank or processing company can help you stay updated, and the credit card companies themselves offer a lot of information about protecting yourself and your customers.

Online merchants have to be wary about hackers, skimmers and common thieves who may use stolen credit card numbers to steal from you. The first step to take to protect yourself is to be sure that you follow the procedures recommended by the card companies and by your payment processor. If you don't, you risk not only being ripped off, but also losing the privilege of accepting credit cards at all.

Try to review each credit card transaction personally, or have someone else do it.

Some warning signs of a fraudulent transaction

- a buyer who uses a free or anonymous e-mail service
- different ship-to and bill-to addresses
- orders or shipments from or to foreign countries
- information that is entered in all lower case (no capital letters used)
- multiples of the same item
- orders that are larger than normal
- high-dollar value orders
- rush orders

There are legitimate reasons for buyers to place orders that fall into any of the above categories, but several of these warning signals in one order may spell a fraudulent transaction.

To further ensure the legitimacy of a transaction

◆ Have the buyer give you the CVV2 number (the three-digit number to the right of the printed card number in the signature panel). If someone is attempting to defraud you, asking for this number is a deterrent, even if your processing system doesn't require it. Legitimate customers will be able to provide the CVV2 numbers if they are holding the card at that moment. Keep in mind that the use of the CVV2 number is effective almost 80 percent of the time, but it is not 100-percent infallible.

◆ If the "ship-to" and "bill-to" names and/or addresses are different, trace the IP number through a service such as VisualWare.com's VisualRoute, which can identify the geographical location of routers, servers, and other IP devices. By using an IP trace, you can compare the geographical origin of the order to the cardholder information. If they are different, it may indicate fraud.

◆ Use a reverse directory to cross-reference the cardholder's telephone number and address. If the cardholder is unlisted, you won't be able to verify this information, but many times you can get an idea of whether the cardholder actually exists and whether he lives where he claims to. Remember that cross-referencing is another verification tool, but it is not infallible.

◆ Use the address verification service from Visa, MasterCard or American Express to verify the cardholder's address. Credit card processing companies also provide address verification services, but there is a lag time between when the credit card company or the credit card issuer receives any information update and when the processing company gets it.

If you follow all the procedures but are still defrauded, you may be able to recoup your money if you have been scrupulous about keeping a paper trail. As with face-to-face card transactions, maintain records of all credit card purchases for several months in case you are called upon to prove your diligence.

As with other types of fraud, an e-commerce insurance rider on your policy may protect you. Discuss this issue with your insurance agent before embarking on Internet sales.

Protect Your Customers Against Online Fraud

Just as you want to be protected against online fraudsters, you owe your customers the peace of mind that comes with being able to place a secure transaction with your business. It is in your best interest to protect buyers, not only for the repeat business, but because you are responsible for your customers' online security when they are on your site.

You will need to speak with your systems administrator regarding the technology that is available to you in order to keep the information in your computer safe. If you are conducting business online, your Web site is vulnerable to hackers, who may want to penetrate your site in order to collect your customers' credit card numbers and other personal information, which can then be used to defraud other merchants.

There are many computer safeguards available, but unfortunately, a lot of systems administrators aren't aware of them, don't know how to use them properly, or simply don't take the time to run the programs. If the lack of knowledge is a problem, invest the time and money necessary to get yourself or your computer expert up to speed – then insist that the safeguards be put into place and the programs run on a regular basis and as needed. It's pointless to have the technological capabilities to protect yourself and your customers if you don't use them. Take advantage of firewalls, encryption techniques, and whatever else is available.

If e-commerce is new to your staff, consult with companies or individuals that have a proven track record in this area and have them help you develop the best computer security plan possible. As with other aspects of security, if you wait until something happens, you will regret not taking action in advance.

Chapter 18
WHAT'S NEXT?

No one can be certain what the future of retail security holds, but some clues can be gleaned from the signals large stores are sending. As more emphasis is put on security measures in the corporate world in general, retailers are following the trend by inaugurating or beefing up existing security procedures.

Looking into the Crystal Ball

The tragedy of September 11, 2001, has affected everyone in some way, and businesses are no exception. One of the biggest impacts September 11 has had on corporations is that security functions are being taken much more seriously than before.

In the past, security was treated like the redheaded stepchild of the corporate world. It was often the first place to cut in times of economic strife and the last to win any respect. Security managers have been hampered in doing their jobs because upper management often failed to support their efforts.

Now big business is reevaluating the importance of corporate security. Today, security managers are receiving larger budgets as well as the backing of top executives. This newfound recognition of the importance of the security function in the corporate world is starting to make its way into the overall consciousness of business in general.

It is likely that this trend will continue in the future. Unfortunately, disasters and tragedies have always existed and will continue to befall us. Therefore, there will always be a need for protection of people and assets. Mom-and-pop stores are just as likely to suffer catastrophes as large retail chains, so the need for preparation is important across the board. Security experts are the natural leaders in this area. As their influence grows in the corporate sphere, it is likely that smaller business concerns will follow in their footsteps and take security more seriously.

Even stores that don't have a budget for professional security services will have to find a way to safeguard their livelihoods. In many cases, the only person who can take on this task is the store owner. Now that proprietors' eyes have been opened, they will have to inform themselves of what they need to do and implement sound plans.

Another reason that corporate policies are changing is because of litigation.

Stores are increasingly focusing on internal theft for a variety of reasons. As the potential liability of stores that employ armed guards has grown steadily, unarmed security personnel has almost completely replaced those with weapons. Now the movement is towards restricting the actions of security personnel who are doing job-related activities, such as apprehending shoplifters, in an attempt to minimize the employer's liabilities.

Some stores, for example, have set a policy that shoplifters are not to be restrained within the store. They have added the restriction that security personnel are not to go past the curb when chasing the thieves, leaving their window of opportunity for catching the bad guys very small. It seems likely that they will be restricted in more ways in the future.

Additionally, human resources are already stretched to the limits in the retail environment, and sending store personnel to court to prosecute shoplifters is a drain the stores are less willing to endure. As a result, the dollar amounts that stores are willing to prosecute for keep increasing. As they increase, more shoplifters are escaping the justice system, let go with only a warning to stay out of the store. They in turn victimize nearby retail establishments, and/or return to the original target store once enough time has elapsed that the turnover in personnel assures that the thieves will not be recognized. Because of these concerns, stores are focusing their attention on internal theft at the expense of external theft.

As economic stresses occur on a large scale, stores feel the impact in several ways. One of them is a change in the policies of banks that process credit cards. Until recently, it was of no concern to a merchant who accepted a bad credit card for a purchase because the bank would wind up eating the charge. Now banks have tightened their policies and are scrutinizing every bad charge carefully. If the bank finds that a store was negligent in processing the card, the store will be charged back. It seems likely that this trend will become the norm in the banking industry, forcing retail businesses to implement additional training and pay careful attention to each charge processed in the future.

In addition, issues of workplace violence and employee safety are moving to the forefront as litigation over these issues increases nationwide. Stores are taking steps to prevent estranged spouses, as well as others likely to interfere with the performance of an employee, from entering the store or from bothering an employee once inside the store. Management is also setting policies about inappropriate behavior of employees that is to be reported by other employees in an effort to hold at bay incidences of workers who "go postal."

It seems clear that as external theft is neglected to focus on internal crimes, it is only a matter of time before the rate of external theft increases. And as stores find themselves eating more shrink caused by external theft, the pendulum will one day again swing back, and the emphasis will revert to preventing shrink from outside sources.

Appendix A
OSHA's Sample Workplace Violence Prevention Policy

This policy can be downloaded from OSHA's Web site at http://www.osha-slc.gov/workplace_violence/wrkplace Violence.PartIII.html and personalized for use in your business.

WORKPLACE VIOLENCE PREVENTION PROGRAM
POLICY STATEMENT

(Effective Date for Program)

Our establishment, [Employer Name] is concerned and committed to our employees' safety and health. We refuse to tolerate violence in the workplace and will make every effort to prevent violent incidents from occurring by implementing a Workplace Violence Prevention Program (WPVP). We will provide adequate authority and budgetary resources to responsible parties so that our goals and responsibilities can be met.

All managers and supervisors are responsible for implementing and maintaining our WPVP Program. We encourage employee participation in designing and implementing our program. We require prompt and accurate reporting of all violent incidents whether or not physical injury has occurred. We will not discriminate against victims of workplace violence.

A copy of this Policy Statement and our WPVP Program is readily available to all employees from each manager and supervisor.

Our Program ensures that all employees, including supervisors and managers, adhere to work practices that are designed to make the workplace more secure, and do not engage in verbal threats or physical actions which create a security hazard for others in the workplace.

All employees, including managers and supervisors, are responsible for using safe work practices, for following all directives, policies and procedures, and for assisting in maintaining a safe and secure work environment.

The management of our establishment is responsible for ensuring that all safety and health policies and procedures involving workplace security are clearly communicated and understood by all employees.

Managers and supervisors are expected to enforce the rules fairly and uniformly.

Our Program will be reviewed and updated annually.

WORKPLACE VIOLENCE PREVENTION PROGRAM

THREAT ASSESSMENT TEAM

A Threat Assessment Team will be established and part of their duties will be to assess the vulnerability to workplace violence at our establishment and reach agreement on preventive actions to be taken. They will be responsible for auditing our overall Workplace Violence Program.

The Threat Assessment Team will consist of:

Name:_____ Title:_____Phone:_____

Name:_____ Title:_____Phone:_____

Name:_____ Title:_____Phone:_____

Name:_____ Title:_____Phone:_____

Name:_____ Title:_____Phone:_____

Name:_____ Title:_____Phone:_____

Name:_____ Title:_____Phone:_____

The team will develop employee training programs in violence prevention and plan for responding to acts of violence. They will communicate this plan internally to all employees. The Threat Assessment Team will begin its work by reviewing previous incidents of violence at our workplace. They will analyze and review existing records identifying patterns that may indicate causes and severity of assault incidents and identify changes necessary to correct these hazards. These records include but are not limited to, OSHA 200 logs, past incident reports, medical records, insurance records, workers compensation records, police reports, accident investigations, training records, grievances, minutes of meetings, etc. The team will communicate with similar local businesses and trade associates concerning their experiences with workplace violence.

Additionally, they will inspect the workplace and evaluate the work tasks of all employees to determine the presence of hazards, conditions, operations and other situations with might place our workers at risk of occupational assault incidents. Employees will be surveyed to identify the potential for violent incidents and to identify or confirm the need for improved security measures. These surveys shall be reviewed, updated and distributed as needed or at least once within a two year period.

Periodic inspections to identify and evaluate workplace security hazards and threats of workplace violence will be performed by the following representatives of the Assessment Team, in the following areas of our workplace:

Representative: _____ Area _____

Representative: _____ Area _____

Representative: _____ Area _____

Periodic inspections will be performed according to the following schedule:

_____

Frequency (Daily, weekly, monthly, etc.)

HAZARD ASSESSMENT

On [Date], the Threat Assessment Team completed the hazard assessment. This consisted of a records review, inspection of the workaday and employee survey.

Records Review - The Threat Assessment Team reviewed the following records:

_____   OSHA 200 logs for the last three years

_____   Incident reports

_____   Records of or information compiled for recording of assault incidents or near assault incidents

_____   Insurance records

_____   Police reports

_____   Accident investigations

_____   Training records

_____   Grievances

_____   Other relevant records or information: _____

_____

From these records, we have identified the following issues that need to be addressed:

WORKPLACE SECURITY ANALYSIS

Inspection - The Threat Assessment Team inspected the workplace on [Date]. From this inspection the following issues have been identified:

Review of Tasks - The Threat Assessment Team also reviewed the work tasks of our employees to determine the presence of hazards, conditions, operations and situations which might place workers at risk of occupational assault incidents. The following factors were considered:

Exchange of money with the public

Working alone or in small numbers

Working late at night or early in the morning hours

Working in a high crime area

Guarding valuable property or possessions

Working in community settings

Staffing levels

From this analysis, the following issues have been identified:

WORKPLACE SURVEY

Under the direction of the Threat Assessment Team, we distributed a survey among all of our employees to identify any additional issues that were not noted in the initial stages of the hazard assessment.

From that survey, the following issues have been identified:

WORKPLACE HAZARD CONTROL AND PREVENTION

In order to reduce the risk of workplace violence, the following measures have been recommended:

Engineering Controls and Building and Work Area Design

Management has instituted the following as a result of the workplace security inspection and recommendations made by the Threat Assessment Team:

These changes were completed on [Date].

Policies and Procedures developed as a result of the Threat Assessment Team's recommendations:

TRAINING AND EDUCATION

Training for all employees, including managers and supervisors, was given on [Date]. This training will be repeated every two years.

Training included:

a review and definition of workplace violence;

a full explanation and full description of our program (all employees were given a copy of this program at orientation);

instructions on how to report all incidents including threats and verbal abuse;

methods of recognizing and responding to workplace security hazards;

training on how to identify potential workplace security hazards (such as no lights in parking lot while leaving late at night, unknown person loitering outside the building, etc.)

review of measures that have been instituted in this organization to prevent workplace violence including:

use of security equipment and procedures;

how to attempt to diffuse hostile or threatening situations;

how to summon assistance in case of an emergency or hostage situation;

post-incident procedures, including medical follow-up and the availability of counseling and referral.

Additional specialized training was given to:

Name _____ Department _____ Job Title _____

Name _____ Department _____ Job Title _____

Name _____ Department _____ Job Title _____

This training was conducted by _____ on [Date] and will be repeated every two years.

Trainers will be qualified and knowledgeable. Our trainers are professionals [list type of certification]. At the end of each training session, employees will be asked to evaluate the session and make suggestions on how to improve the training.

All training records will be filed with _____.

Workplace Violence Prevention training will be given to new employees as part of their orientation.

A general review of this program will be conducted every two years. Our training program will be updated to reflect changes in our Workplace Prevention Program.

INCIDENT REPORTING AND INVESTIGATION

All incidents must be reported within [Time]. An "Incident Report Form" will be completed for all incidents. One copy will be forwarded to the Threat Assessment Team for their review and a copy will be filed with [Job Title].

Each incident will be evaluated by the Threat Assessment Team. The team will discuss the causes of the incident and will make recommendations on how to revise the program to prevent similar incidents from occurring. All revisions of the Program will be put into writing and made available to all employees.

RECORD KEEPING

We will maintain an accurate record of all workplace violence incidents. All incident report forms will be kept for a minimum of [Time], or for the time specified in the Statute of Limitations for our local jurisdiction.

Any injury which requires more than first aid, is a lost-time injury, requires modified duty, or causes loss of consciousness, will be recorded on the OSHA 200 log. Doctors' reports and supervisors' reports will be kept of each recorded incident, if applicable.

Incidents of abuse, verbal attack, or aggressive behavior which may be threatening to the employee, but not resulting in injury, will be recorded. These records will be evaluated on a regular basis by the Threat Assessment Team.

Minutes of the Threat Assessment Team meetings shall be kept for [Time].

Records of training program contents, and the sign-in sheets of all attendees, shall be kept for [Time]. Qualifications of the trainers shall be maintained along with the training records.

COMPLETED WPVP PROGRAM (EXAMPLE)

ABC COMPANIES WPVP PROGRAM POLICY STATEMENT
JANUARY 1, 1996

Our establishment, ABC COMPANY, is concerned and committed to our employees' safety and health. We refuse to tolerate violence in the workplace and will make every effort to prevent violent incidents from occurring by implementing a Workplace Violence Prevention Program (WPVP). We will provide adequate authority and budgetary resources to responsible parties so that our goals and responsibilities can be met.

All managers and supervisors are responsible for implementing and maintaining our WPVP Program. We encourage employee participation in designing and implementing our program. We require prompt and accurate reporting of all violent incidents whether or not physical injury has occurred. We will not discriminate against victims of workplace violence.

A copy of this Policy Statement and our WPVP Program is readily available to all employees from each manager and supervisor.

Our Program ensures that all employees, including supervisors and managers, adhere to work practices that are designed to make the workplace more secure, and do not engage in verbal threats or physical actions which create a security hazard for others in the workplace.

All employees, including managers and supervisors, are responsible for using safe work practices, for following all directives, policies and procedures, and for assisting in maintaining a safe and secure work environment.

The management of our establishment is responsible for ensuring that all safety and health policies and procedures involving workplace security are clearly communicated and understood by all employees. Managers and supervisors are expected to enforce the rules fairly and uniformly.

Our Program will be reviewed and updated annually.

WORKPLACE VIOLENCE PREVENTION PROGRAM

THREAT ASSESSMENT TEAM

A Threat Assessment Team will be established and part of their duties will be to assess the vulnerability to workplace violence at our establishment and reach agreement on preventive actions to be taken. They will be responsible for auditing our overall Workplace Violence Program.

The Threat Assessment Team will consist of:

Name: John Smith	Title: Vice President	Phone: 555-1212
Name: Jane Doe	Title: Operations	Phone: 555-1234
Name: Frank Kras	Title: Shop Steward	Phone: 555-1233
Name: James Brown	Title: Security	Phone: 555-1456
Name: Susan Dean	Title: Treasurer	Phone: 555-1567
Name: Tom Jones	Title: Legal Counsel	Phone: 555-1678
Name: Sally Field	Title: Personnel	Phone: 555-1789

The team will develop employee training programs in violence prevention and plan for responding to acts of violence. They will communicate this plan internally to all employees.

The Threat Assessment Team will begin its work by reviewing previous incidents of violence at our workplace. They will analyze and review existing records identifying patterns that may indicate causes and severity of assault incidents and identify changes necessary to correct these hazards. These records include but are not limited to, OSHA 200 logs, past incident reports, medical records, insurance records, workers compensation records, police reports, accident investigations, training records, grievances, minutes of meetings, etc. The team will communicate with similar local businesses and trade associates concerning their experiences with workplace violence.

Additionally, they will inspect the workplace and evaluate the work tasks of all employees to determine the presence of hazards, conditions, operations and other situations which might place our workers at risk of occupational assault incidents. Employees will be surveyed to identify the potential for violent incidents and to identify or confirm the need for improved security measures. These surveys shall be reviewed, updated and distributed as needed or at least once within a two year period.

Periodic inspections to identify and evaluate workplace security hazards and threats of workplace violence will be performed by the following representatives of the Assessment Team, in the following areas of our workplace:

Representative: John Smith   Area: General Office

Representative: Frank Kras   Area: Shop and Lab

Representative: Jane Doe   Area: Reception & Sales

Periodic inspections will be performed according to the following schedule:

First Monday of Every Month _____
Frequency (Daily, weekly, monthly, etc.)

HAZARD ASSESSMENT

On September 5, 1995, the Threat Assessment Team completed the hazard assessment. This consisted of a records review, inspection of the worksite and employee survey.

Records Review - The Threat Assessment Team reviewed the following records:

___X___ OSHA 200 logs for the last three years

___X___ Incident reports

___X___ Records of or information compiled for recording of assault incidents or near assault incidents

___X___ Insurance records

_____ Police reports

_____ Accident investigations

_____ Training records

___X___ Grievances

___X___ Other relevant records or information: Workers' Compensation records.

From these records, we have identified the following issues that need to be addressed:

employees have been assaulted by irate clients;

employees have been assaulted while traveling alone;

there have been several incidents of assault and harassment among employees.

WORKPLACE SECURITY ANALYSIS

Inspection - The Threat Assessment Team inspected the workplace on July 31, 1995.

From this inspection the following issues have been identified:

access to the building is not controlled; and it is not limited to any of the offices on the four floors that we occupy. There have been problems with non-employees entering private work areas;

doors to the restrooms are not kept locked;

lighting in the parking lot is inadequate;

in client service area, desks are situated in a way that make it necessary for employees to walk past the client in order to leave area. There are many objects on top of desks that could be used as weapons (i.e., scissors, stapler, file rack, etc.).

Review of Tasks - The Threat Assessment Team also reviewed the work tasks of our employees to determine the presence of hazards, conditions, operations and situations which might place workers at risk of occupational assault incidents. The following factors were considered:

Exchange of money with the public

Working alone or in small numbers

Working late at night or early in the morning hours

Working in a high crime area

Guarding valuable property or possessions

Working in community settings

Staffing levels

From this analysis, the following issues have been identified:

employees in client service area exchange money with clients;

there are several employees who work very late hours or come in very early in the morning in the shop and lab areas.

WORKPLACE SURVEY

Under the direction of the Threat Assessment Team, we distributed a survey among all of our employees to identify any additional issues that were not noted in the initial stages of the hazard assessment. From that survey, the following issues have been identified:

employees who work in the field have experienced threats of violence on several occasions, and there have been several near miss incidents. Employees noted that they were unsure of how to handle the situation and that they are often afraid to travel by themselves to areas they perceive are dangerous;

employees who work directly with clients in the office have also experienced threats, both verbal and physical, from some of the clients.

WORKPLACE HAZARD CONTROL AND PREVENTION

In order to reduce the risk of workplace violence, the following measures have been recommended:

Engineering Controls and Building and Work Area Design

Employees who have client contact in the facility, will have their work areas designed to ensure that they are protected from possible threats from their clients.

Changes to be completed as soon as possible include:

arranging desks and chairs to prevent entrapment of the employees;

removing items from the top of desks, such as scissors, staplers, etc. that can be used as a weapon;

installing panic buttons to assist employees when they are threatened by clients. The buttons can be activated by one's foot. The signal will be transmitted to a supervisor's desk, as well as the security desk, which is always staffed.

Management has instituted the following as a result of the workplace security inspection and recommendations made by the Threat Assessment Team:

Installation of plexi-glass payment window for employees who handle money and need to take payments from clients (number of employees who take money will be strictly limited);

Adequate lighting systems installed for indoor building areas as well as areas around the outside of the facility and in the parking areas. The lighting systems will be maintained on a regular basis to ensure safety to all employees;

Locks installed on restroom doors. Keys will be given to each department. Restroom doors are to be kept locked at all times. Supervisors will ensure that the keys are returned to ensure continued security for employees in their areas.

Installation of panic buttons in employees' work areas.

Memorandum to all employees requesting that they remove any items from their desks that can be used as a weapon, such as scissors, staplers, etc.

These changes were completed by January 1, 1996.

Policies and Procedures developed as a result of the Threat Assessment Team recommendations:

Employees who are required to work in the field and who feel that the situation is unsafe should travel in "buddy" systems or with an escort from their supervisor.

Employees who work in the field will report to their supervisor periodically throughout the day. They will be provided with a personal beeper or cellular phone, which will allow them to contact assistance should an incident occur.

Access to the building will be controlled. All employees have been given a name badge which is to be worn at all times. If employees come in early, or are working past 7:30 p.m., they must enter and exit through the main entrance.

Visitors will be required to sign in at the front desk. All clients must enter through the main entrance to gain access.

TRAINING AND EDUCATION

Training for all employees, including managers and supervisors, was given on September 11, 1995. This training will be repeated every two years.

Training included:

a review and definition of workplace violence;

a full explanation and full description of our program (all employees were given a copy of this program at orientation);

instructions on how to report all incidents including threats and verbal abuse;

methods of recognizing and responding to workplace security hazards;

training on how to identify potential workplace security hazards (such as no lights in parking lot while leaving late at night, unknown person loitering outside the building, etc.)

review of measures that have been instituted in this organization to prevent workplace violence including

use of security equipment and procedures;

how to attempt to diffuse hostile or threatening situations;

how to summon assistance in case of an emergency or hostage situation;

post-incident procedures, including medical follow-up and the availability of counseling and referral.

Additional specialized training was given to

Employees who work in the field;

Employees who handle money with clients;

Employees who work after hours or come in early.

Specialized training included

Personal safety;

Importance of the buddy system;

Recognizing unsafe situations and how to handle them during off hours.

This training was conducted by in-house staff, with assistance from the local police department on October 1, 1995 and will be repeated every two years.

Trainers were qualified and knowledgeable. Our trainers are professionals certified by ASIS International.

At the end of each training session, employees are asked to evaluate the session and make suggestions on how to improve the training.

All training records are filed with the Human Resource Department/ Personnel Department.

Workplace Violence Prevention training will be given to new employees as part of their orientation.

A general review of this program will be conducted every two years. Our training program will be updated to reflect changes in our Workplace Prevention Program.

INCIDENT REPORTING AND INVESTIGATION

All incidents must be reported within four (4) hours. An "Incident Report Form" will be completed for all incidents. One copy will be forwarded to the Threat Assessment Team for their review and a copy will be filed with the Human Resource/Personnel Department.

Each incident will be evaluated by the Threat Assessment Team. The team will discuss the causes of the incident and will make recommendations on how to revise the program to prevent similar incidents from occurring. All revisions of the Program will be put into writing and made available to all employees.

RECORDKEEPING

We will maintain an accurate record of all workplace violence incidents. All incident report forms will be kept for a minimum of seven (7) years, or for the time specified in the statute of limitations for our local jurisdiction.

Any injury which requires more than first aid, is a lost-time injury, requires modified duty, or causes loss of consciousness, will be recorded on the OSHA 200 log. Doctors' reports and supervisors' reports will be kept of each recorded incident, if applicable.

Incidents of abuse, verbal attack, or aggressive behavior which may be threatening to the employee, but not resulting in injury, will be recorded. These records will be evaluated on a regular basis by the Threat Assessment Team.

Minutes of the Threat Assessment Team meetings shall be kept for three (3) years.

Records of training program contents, and the sign-in sheets of all attendees, shall be kept for five (5) years. Qualifications of the trainers shall be maintained along with the training records.

SELF INSPECTION SECURITY CHECKLIST

Facility: _____

Inspector: _____

Date of Inspection: _____

1. Security Control Plan: Yes   No

    If yes, does it contain

    (A) Policy statement   Yes   No

    (B) Review of employee incident exposure   Yes   No

    (C) Methods of control   Yes   No

        If yes, does it include

        Engineering   Yes   No

        Work practice   Yes   No

        Training   Yes   No

        Reporting procedures   Yes   No

        Recordkeeping   Yes   No

        Counseling   Yes   No

    (D) Evaluation of incidents   Yes   No

    (E) Floor plan   Yes   No

    (F) Protection of assets   Yes   No

    (G) Computer security   Yes   No

    (H) Plan accessible to all employees   Yes   No

    (I) Plan reviewed and updated annually   Yes   No

    (J) Plan reviewed and updated when tasks are
        added or changed   Yes   No

2. Policy statement by employer   Yes   No

3. Work areas evaluated by employer   Yes   No

   If yes, how often? _____

4. Engineering controls   Yes   No
   If yes, does it include
   (A) Mirrors to see around corners and in blind spots   Yes   No
   (B) Landscaping to provide unobstructed view of the workplace

                                                      Yes   No
   (C) "Fishbowl effect" to allow unobstructed view of the interior

                                                      Yes   No
   (D) Limiting the posting of sale signs on windows   Yes   No
   (E) Adequate lighting in and around the workplace   Yes   No
   (F) Parking lot well lighted   Yes   No
   (G) Door control(s)   Yes   No
   (H) Panic button(s)   Yes   No
   (I) Door detector(s)   Yes   No
   (J) Closed circuit TV   Yes   No
   (K) Stationary metal detector   Yes   No
   (L) Sound detection   Yes   No
   (M) Intrusion detection system   Yes   No
   (N) Intrusion panel   Yes   No
   (O) Monitor(s)   Yes   No
   (P) Video tape recorder   Yes   No
   (Q) Switcher   Yes   No
   (R) Handheld metal detector   Yes   No
   (S) Handheld video camera   Yes   No
   (T) Personnel traps ("Sally Traps")   Yes   No
   (U) Other _____   Yes   No

5. Structural Modifications

    Plexiglas, glass guard, wire glass, partitions, etc.   Yes   No

    If yes, comment:_____

    _____

6. Security guards   Yes   No

    (A) If yes, are there an appropriate number for the site?

    Yes   No

    (B) Are they knowledgeable of the company WPVP Policy?

    Yes   No

    (C) Indicate if they are

    ___Contract Guards (1) ___In-house Employees (2)

    (D) At entrance(s)   Yes   No

    (E) Building patrol   Yes   No

    (F) Guards provided with communication?   Yes   No

        If yes, indicate what type: _____

    (G) Guards receive training on Workplace Violence situations?

    Yes   No

        Comments: _____

        _____

7. Work practice controls   Yes   No

    If yes, indicate:_____

    (A) Desks clear of objects which may become missiles   Yes   No

    (B) Unobstructed office exits   Yes   No

    (C) Vacant (bare) cubicles available   Yes   No

    (D) Reception area available   Yes   No

    (E) Visitor/client sign in/out   Yes   No

    (F) Visitor(s)/client(s) escorted   Yes   No

(G) Barriers to separate clients from work area   Yes   No

(H) One entrance used   Yes   No

(I) Separate interview area(s)   Yes   No

(J) I.D. Badges used   Yes   No

(K) Emergency numbers posted by phones   Yes   No

(L) Internal phone system   Yes   No

   If yes, indicate: Does it use 120 VAC Building Lines? Yes   No

   Does it use phone lines?   Yes   No

(M) Internal procedures for conflict (problem) situations

                                                       Yes   No

(N) Procedures for employee dismissal   Yes   No

(O) Limit spouse & family visits to designated areas   Yes   No

(P) Key control procedures   Yes   No

(Q) Access control to the workplace   Yes   No

(R) Objects which may become missiles removed from area

                                                       Yes   No

(S) Parking prohibited in Fire Zones   Yes   No

Other:_____

_____

7a. Off Premises Work Practice Controls (For staff who work away from
     a fixed workplace, such as social services, real estate, utilities, police/
     fire/sanitation, taxi/limo, construction, sales/delivery, messengers, and
     others.)

(A) Trained in hazardous situation avoidance   Yes   No

(B) Briefed about areas where they work   Yes   No

(C) Have reviewed past incidents by type and area   Yes   No

(D) Know directions and routes for day's schedule   Yes   No

(E) Previewed client/case histories   Yes   No

(F) Left an itinerary with contact information   Yes   No

(G) Have periodic check-in procedures   Yes   No

(H) After hours contact procedures   Yes   No

(I) Partnering arrangements if deemed necessary   Yes   No

(J) Know how to control/defuse potentially violent situations

                                                         Yes   No

(K) Supplied with personal alarm/cellular phone/radio Yes   No

(L) Limit visible clues of carrying money/valuables   Yes   No

(M) Carry forms to record incidents by area   Yes   No

(N) Know procedures if involved in incident   Yes   No

                                        (see also Training Section)

8. Training conducted   Yes   No

    If yes, is it

    (A) Prior to initial assignment   Yes   No

    (B) At least annually thereafter   Yes   No

    (C) Does it include

        Components of security control plan   Yes   No

        Engineering and workplace controls instituted at workplace

                                                         Yes   No

        Techniques to use in potentially volatile situations

                                                         Yes   No

        How to anticipate/read behavior   Yes   No

        Procedures to follow after an incident   Yes   No

        Periodic refresher for on-site procedures   Yes   No

        Recognizing abuse/paraphernalia   Yes   No

        Opportunity for Q and A with instructor   Yes   No

        Hazards unique to job tasks   Yes   No

9. Written training records kept   Yes   No

10. Are incidents reported   Yes   No

    If yes, are they

    (A) Reported in written form   Yes   No

    (B) First report of injury form (if employee loses time) Yes   No

11. Incidents evaluated   Yes   No

    (A) EAP counseling offered   Yes   No

    (B) Other action (reporting requirements, suggestions, reporting to

        local authorities, etc.) _____

        _____

    (C) Are steps taken to prevent recurrence?   Yes   No

12. Floor Plans Posted Showing Exits, Entrances, Location of Security

    Equipment, Etc.   Yes   No

    If yes, does it

        Include an emergency action plan, evacuation plan, and/or a

        disaster contingency plan?   Yes   No

13. Do employees feel safe?   Yes   No

    (A) Have employees been surveyed to find out their concerns?

                                                                                Yes   No

    (B) Has the employer utilized the crime prevention services and/or

        lectures provided by the local or state police?   Yes   No

Comments: _____

_____

General comments/recommendations: _____

_____

INCIDENT REPORT FORM

1. Victim's name:_____ Job Title:_____

2. Victim's address: _____

3. Home phone number:_____ Work phone number: _____

4. Employer's name and address: _____

5. Department/section: _____

6. Victim's Social Security number: _____

7. Incident date _____

8. Incident time: _____

9. Incident location: _____

10. Work location (if different):_____

11. Type of incident (circle one):

    assault   robbery   harassment

    disorderly conduct   sex offense

    other   (Please specify)

    _____

    (See attached - DEFINITION OF INCIDENTS WORKSHEET)

12. Were you injured? (circle):   Yes   No

    If yes, please specify your injuries and the location of any treatment:

    _____

    _____

    _____

    _____

    _____

13. Did police respond to incident?   Yes   No

14. What police department: _____

15. Police report filed: Yes   No
    Report Number: _____

16. Was your supervisor notified?   Yes   No

17. Supervisor's name: _____

18. Was the local union/employee representative notified? Yes   No
    Who should be notified _____

19. Was any action taken by employer: (specify) _____
_____

20. Assailant/perpetrator (circle one):

    Intruder   Customer   Patient   Resident   Client
    Visitor   Student   Co-Worker   Former Employee
    Supervisor   Family/Friend
    Other (specify): _____
_____

21. Assailant/perpetrator - Name/Address/Age (if known): _____
_____
_____

22. Please, briefly describe the incident:
_____
_____
_____

23. Incident disposition (circle all that apply):

    No action taken   Arrest   Warning

    Suspension   Reprimand   Other _____

    _____

24. Did the incident involve a weapon: Yes   No

    Specify _____

    _____

25. Did you lose any work days?   Yes   No

    Specify _____

    _____

26. Were you singled out or was the violence directed at more than one individual?

    Specify_____

    _____

27. Were you alone when the incident occurred?   Yes   No

28. Did you have any reason to believe that an incident might occur?

                                                          Yes   No

    Why? _____

29. Has this type or similar incident(s) happened to you or your co-workers?   Yes   No

    Specify: _____

30. Have you had any counseling or support since the incident?

                                                       Yes   No

    Specify: _____

31. What do you feel can be done in the future to avoid such an incident?_____

_____

32. Was this assailant involved in previous incidents?_____

_____

33. Are there any measures in place to prevent similar incidents?

                                                       Yes   No

    Specify:_____

34. Has corrective action been taken?

    Specify: _____

35. Comments: _____

_____

_____

_____

_____

_____

_____

_____

SAMPLE EMPLOYEE SECURITY SURVEY

This survey will help detect security problems in your building or at an alternate worksite.

Please fill out this form, get your co-workers to fill it out and review it to see where the potential for major security problems lie.

NAME: _____

WORK LOCATION: _____
(IN BUILDING OR ALTERNATE WORKSITE)

1. Do either of these two conditions exist in your building or at your alternate work site?
    ___ Work alone during working hours.
    ___ No notification given to anyone when you finish work.
    Are these conditions a problem? If so when, please describe. (For example, Mondays, evening, daylight savings time)

2. Do you have any of the following complaints (that may be associated with causing an unsafe worksite)? (Check all that apply)
    ___ Does your workplace have a written policy to follow for addressing general problems?
    ___ Does your workplace have a written policy on how to handle a violent client?
    ___ When and how to request the assistance of a co-worker
    ___ When and how to request the assistance of police
    ___ What to do about a verbal threat
    ___ What to do about a threat of violence
    ___ What to do about harassment
    ___ Working alone
    ___ Alarm System(s)
    ___ Security in and out of building
    ___ Security in parking lot

___ Have you been assaulted by a co-worker?

___ To your knowledge have incidents of violence ever occurred between your co-workers?

3. Are violence related incidents worse during shift work, on the road or in other situations?

   Please specify: _____

4. Where in the building or work site would a violence related incident most likely occur?

   ____ lounge ____ exits ____ deliveries ____ private offices

   ____ parking lot ____ bathroom ____ entrance ____ Other

   Other (specify)_____

5. Have you ever noticed a situation that could lead to a violent incident?

6. Have you missed work because of a potential violent act(s) committed during your course of employment?

7. Do you receive workplace violence related training or assistance of any kind?

8. Has anything happened recently at your worksite that could have led to violence?

9. Can you comment about the situation?

10. Has the number of violent clients increased?

Definition of Incidents

ASSAULT: The intentional use of physical injury, (impairment of physical condition or substantial pain) to another person, with or without a weapon or dangerous instrument.

CRIMINAL MISCHIEF: Intentional or reckless damaging of the property of another person without permission.

DISORDERLY CONDUCT: Intentionally causing public inconvenience, annoyance or alarm or recklessly creating a risk thereof by fighting (without injury) or in violent, numinous or threatening behavior or making unreasonable noise, shouting abuse, misbehaving, disturbing an assembly or meeting or persons or creating hazardous conditions by an act which serves no legitimate purpose.

HARASSMENT: Intentionally striking, shoving or kicking another or subjecting another person to physical contact, or threatening to do the same (without physical injury). ALSO, using abusive or obscene language or following a person about in a public place, or engaging in a course of conduct which alarms or seriously annoys another person.

LARCENY: Wrongful taking, depriving or withholding property from another (no force involved). Victim may or may not be present.

MENACING: Intentionally places or attempts to place another person in fear of imminent serious physical injury.

RECKLESS ENDANGERMENT: Subjecting individuals to danger by recklessly engaging in conduct which creates substantial risk of serious physical injury.

ROBBERY: Forcible stealing of another's property by use of threat of immediate physical force. (Victim is present and aware of theft.)

SEX OFFENSE:
Criminal Sexual Act: A deviant sexual act committed, as in rape.
Public Lewdness: Exposure of sexual organs to others.
Sexual Abuse: Subjecting another to sexual contact without consent.
Rape: Sexual intercourse without consent.

Appendix B
MODEL SEXUAL HARASSMENT POLICY

his model policy is based on the one used by the National Institute of Standards and Technology (NIST). NIST is an agency of the U.S. Commerce Department's Technology Administration.

It is NIST policy that all employees must be allowed to work in an environment free from unsolicited and unwelcome verbal or physical sexual advances. Sexual harassment is a form of unlawful conduct which undermines the integrity of the employment relationship. Therefore, it is NIST's position that sexual harassment is unacceptable conduct in the workplace and will not be tolerated. Complaints and determinations of sexual harassment will be examined through the NIST's EEO complaint process. Violations of this policy can result in legal action.

PURPOSE

The purpose of this policy is to remove from the working environment activities of a sexual nature which create an intimidating, hostile, or offensive work environment or impede the ability of a person to perform a job. In addition, this policy serves to create an atmosphere which allows and encourages those who may be the victims of harassment to first inform the person indulging in the harassment that the action is offensive. If the harassment continues, then the complaint process should be used to address this form of conduct. The scope of activities that this policy addresses can range from harassment as a result of joking to cases of soliciting sexual favors.

BACKGROUND

Harassment on the basis of sex is a violation of Title VII of the Civil Rights Act of 1964, as amended. Because of the continued prevalence of this unlawful practice, the Equal Employment Opportunity Commission (EEOC) has issued guidelines to assist in the efforts to curtail sexual harassment. Based on and consistent with the EEOC Guidelines on Sexual Harassment, NIST in its role as an employer has taken the position of seeking to eliminate sexual harassment from the workplace.

DEFINITION

Sexual harassment is any unsolicited or unwelcome verbal comment, gesture, or physical contact of a sexual nature. Criteria to be used in determining whether an action constitutes unlawful behavior are as follows:

1. Submission to sexually harassing conduct is either an explicit or implicit term or condition of employment.

2. Submission to or rejection of sexually harassing conduct is used as the basis to control, influence, or affect the job, salary, or career of an employee.

3. Sexually harassing conduct has the purpose or effect of interfering with work performance or creating an intimidating, hostile, or offensive work environment.

RESPONSIBILITIES

Office of Human Resources Management will incorporate the NIST policy against sexual harassment into the employee orientation program and as a mandatory element for internal supervisory and management training.

Managers and supervisors are held accountable for enforcing standards of appropriate office behavior and are expected to take prompt action to deal with any conduct identified as sexual harassment under this policy.

Employees will comply with the NIST policy against sexual harassment. In addition, employees who feel that they are victims of sexual harassment have several avenues of redress. They may confront the harasser, or seek help from their supervisor or higher level official who will promptly handle the matter. They may also initiate a discrimination complaint by contacting an EEO Counselor within 45 days of the harassment, report it to the Department of Commerce's Office of Inspector General, or report it as a prohibited personnel practice to the Office of Special Counsel.

Appendix C
SECURITY RESOURCES

CANADIAN RESOURCES

Canadian Bankers Association
Box 348
Commerce Court West
199 Bay Street, 30th Floor
Toronto, ON M5L 1G2
(800) 263-0231 or (416) 362-6092
Fax: (416) 362-7705
E-mail: inform@cba.ca
www.cba.ca

Canadian Council of Better Business Bureaus
44 Byward Market Square, Suite 220
Ottawa, ON K1N 7A2
(613) 789-5151
Fax: (613) 789-7044
E-Mail: ccbbb@canadiancouncilbbb.ca
www.canadiancouncilbbb.ca

Canadian Federation of Independent Business
4141 Yonge Street, Suite 401
Willowdale, ON M2P 2A6
(416) 222-8022
Fax: (416) 222-7593
E-Mail: cfib@cfib.ca
www.cfib.ca

Insurance Bureau of Canada
151 Yonge Street, Suite 1800
Toronto, ON M5C 2W7
(416) 362-2031
Fax: (416) 361-5952
E-Mail: consumercentre@ibc.ca
www.ibc.ca

Workers' Compensation Board of British Columbia
(WorkSafe BC)
P.O. Box 5350, Stn. Terminal
Vancouver, BC V6B 5L5
(888) 922-2768 or (604) 244-6181
Fax: (604) 244-6490
www.worksafebc.com

CREDIT CARDS, CHECKS AND TRAVELERS CHECKS

American Express Company
200 Vesey Street
New York, NY 10285-4814
(212) 640-5130
Credit Cards: (800) 528-5200
Suspect Credit Card Fraud (Report a "Code 10"): (800) 528-2121
Travelers Cheques: (800) 525-7641
www.americanexpress.com

Discover Financial Services
2121 Waukegan Rd
Deerfield, IL 60015-1827
(800) 347-1111 or (801) 902-3100
www.discoverbiz.com

MasterCard International
2000 Purchase Street
Purchase, NY 10577-2405
(800) 300-3069 or (914) 249-2000
Fax: (914) 249-4207
www.mastercard.com

National Check Fraud Center
P.O. Box 80171
Charleston, SC 29414
(843) 571-2143
Fax: (843) 571-4349
E-Mail: cbruce@ckfraud.org
www.ckfraud.org

PayPal
303 Bryant Street
Mountain View, CA 94041
(402) 935-2050
www.paypal.com

TeleCheck
5251 Westheimer Rd
Houston, TX 77056-5412
(800) 835-3243 or (713) 331-7600
www.telecheck.com

Visa U.S.A.
P.O. Box 194607
San Francisco, CA 94119-4607
(415) 932-2100
Credit Cards: (800) 428-1858
Travelers Cheques: (800) 227-6811
E-Mail: AskVisa@Visa.com
www.visa.com

CRIME PREVENTION AND SECURITY

ADT Security Services
One Town Center Road
Boca Raton, FL 33483
(800) 500-4943 or (561) 988-3600
E-Mail: tfssinfo$@tycoint.com
    www.adt.com

ASIS International (American Society for Industrial Security)
1625 Prince Street
Alexandria, VA 22314-2818
(703) 519-6200
Fax: (703) 519-6299
E-Mail: asis@asisonline.org
www.asisonline.org

Liz Martínez Retail Crime and Loss Prevention Training
(718) 389-5184
(773) 481-4964 - Contact: Buhrmaster Consulting Group
E-Mail: hozro@hotmail.com
www.retailsecurity.biz

189 National Crime Prevention Council
1000 Connecticut Avenue, NW, 13th Floor
Washington, DC 20036
(202) 466-6272
Fax: (202) 296-1356
www.ncpc.org

Sensormatic
One Town Center Road
Boca Raton, FL 33483
(561) 988-7200
E-Mail: tfssinfo$@tycoint.com
www.sensormatic.com

State Patrol and State Police Agencies Directory
www.statetroopersdirectory.com

FINANCIAL AGENCIES AND ASSOCIATIONS

American Bankers Association
1120 Connecticut Avenue, NW
Washington, DC 20036
(800) BANKERS or (202) 663-5000
E-Mail: custserv@aba.com
www.aba.com

Federal Reserve Board
20th Street and Constitution Avenue, NW
Washington, DC 20551
(202) 452-3000
www.federalreserve.gov

Check Payment Systems Association
2025 M Street, NW, Suite 800
Washington, DC 20036-3309
(202) 367-1144
Fax: (202) 367-2144
E-Mail: info@cpsa-checks.org
www.cpsa-checks.org

The Department of the Treasury
Bureau of Engraving and Printing
14th & C Streets, SW
Washington, DC 20228
(202) 874-3019
www.newmoney.com

U.S. Secret Service
950 H Street, N.W., Suite 8400
Washington, DC 20223
(202) 406-5708
www.secretservice.gov

INSURANCE

National Association of Insurance Commissioners
2301 McGee Street, Suite 800
Kansas City, MO 64108-2662
(816) 842-3600
Fax: (816) 783-8175
www.naic.org

PUBLICATIONS

Looseleaf Law Publications
43-08 162nd Street
Flushing, NY 11358
(800) 647-5547 or (718) 359-5559
Fax: (718) 539-0941
E-Mail: llawpub@erols.com
www.looseleaflaw.com

LossPrevention **Magazine**
7436 Leharne Drive
Charlotte, NC 28270
(704) 365-5226
Fax: (704) 365-1026
E-Mail: comments@LossPreventionMagazine.com
www.LossPreventionMagazine.com

National Retail Security Survey
University of Florida, Dept. of Sociology
3219 Turlington Hall
P.O. Box 117330
Gainesville, FL 32611-7330
(352) 392-0265
Fax: (352) 392-6568
E-Mail: rhollin@soc.ufl.edu
http://web.soc.ufl.edu/srp.htm

Retail Security Free E-Newsletter
E-Mail: hozro@hotmail.com
www.RetailSecurity.biz

Security Technology & Design **Magazine**
100 Colony Park Drive, Suite 203
Cumming, GA 30040
(770) 886-0800
Fax: (770) 889-7703
http://www.simon-net.com/st-and-d

RETAIL ASSOCIATIONS AND ORGANIZATIONS

Council of Better Business Bureaus
4200 Wilson Boulevard, Suite 800
Arlington, VA 22203-1838
(703) 276-0100
Fax: (703) 525-8277
www.bbb.org

Merchant Risk Council
(512) 977-5422
E-Mail: info@merchantriskcouncil.org
www.merchantriskcouncil.org

National Retail Federation
325 7th Street NW, Suite 1100
Washington DC 20004
(800) NRF-HOW2 or (202) 783-7971
Fax: 202-737-2849
www.nrf.com

WORKPLACE COMPLIANCE AND SAFETY

National Institute for Occupational Safety and Health (NIOSH)
Hubert H. Humphrey Building
200 Independence Ave., SW, Room 715H
Washington, DC 20201
(800) 35-NIOSH or (513) 533-8328
Fax: (513) 533-8573
www.cdc.gov/niosh

Occupational Safety and Health Administration (OSHA)
U.S. Department of Labor
200 Constitution Avenue, NW
Washington, D.C. 20210
(202) 693-2000
www.osha.gov

U.S. Commission on Civil Rights
624 Ninth Street, NW
Washington, DC 20425
(202) 376-8128
www.usccr.gov

INDEX

OTHER TITLES OF INTEREST
FROM LOOSELEAF LAW PUBLICATIONS, INC.

Klein's Uniform Firearms Policy
A Manual for Private Sector Detectives and Security Agents
by Chuck Klein

The "HOW" of Criminal Law
by Francis M. Conlon

Defensive Living
*Attitudes, Tactics and Proper Handgun Use to Secure
Your Personal Well-Being*
by Ed Lovette & Dave Spaulding

**Essential Guide to Handguns for Personal Defense and
Protection**
by Steven R. Rementer and Bruce M. Eimer, Ph.D.

Retail Theft Reports Program CD-ROM
by Angelo deLeon

Bad Check Recovery Program CD-ROM
by Angelo deLeon

**Identity Theft First Responder Manual for Criminal Justice
Professionals** – *Includes Free Victims' Assistance Guide*
by Judith M. Collins, Ph.D. and
Sandra K. Hoffman, B.A.

The *New* Dictionary of Legal Terms
by Irving Shapiro

Police Officer Examination
Preparation Guide
by Larry F. Jetmore

Path of the Warrior
*An Ethical Guide to Personal & Professional
Development in the Field of Criminal Justice*
by Larry F. Jetmore

(800) 647-5547   **www.LooseleafLaw.com**

Retail Theft Reports Program

Reporting incidents of retail theft and shoplifting to the police has never been easier!

Spend less time writing and more time apprehending and preventing thefts.

Submit legally correct reports each and every time.

● **Get it right the first time!** ● **Password Protected!**

THREE EASY STEPS

1. Enter information about the accused.
2. Enter stolen items and their values.
3. Choose the appropriate statement.

INCLUDES

Confession Statement ● Evidence Log ● General Release Statement

AUTOMATICALLY GENERATES A
DETAILED REPORT OF
SHOPLIFTING INCIDENTS

STOLEN ITEMS ARE AUTOMATICALLY TOTALED

PROGRAM MAINTAINS A SEARCHABLE
DATABASE OF ALL APPREHENSIONS

Seeing is Believing! - Request our Demo

ISBN 1-889031-42-9 – **$29.95 - One CD-ROM**

IBM Compatible - Uses 4MB of Disk Space